Endorsements

Adoption and the Gospel paints in vibrant co̶ orphans and how ordinary Christians can reflect that love in our lives. It's rich in theology that makes God's true character so very visible and tender. For ultimately we see that God's deep love for the orphan reveals the depth of His love for each of us as well.

—Jedd Medefind, president, Christian Alliance for Orphans and author of *Becoming Home*.

Many Christians around the world have responded to the orphan crisis, but few biblical resources exist to guide this response. This study provides not only a deep dive into the theology of God's heart for the orphan, but through sharing his personal journey from orphanage administrator to director of the Home for Good Foundation, Gerald Clark brings us deep into the heart of the orphan child as well. With vivid insight and refreshing candor, we learn what the orphaned child desires most and how the experience of institutionalization impacts a child's response. This study should be required reading for anyone serving the orphan abroad, planning a mission trip, or planning to adopt.

—Jodi Jackson Tucker, international director, Orphan Sunday, Christian Alliance for Orphans

How can such a simple and profound observation from the Scriptures be so overlooked? There are many passages that speak about our adoption as beloved children into the family of God, yet even in my four years at Dallas Theological Seminary, I don't recall ever hearing this doctrine emphasized. *Adoption and the Gospel* is a real eye-opener that examines God's design in using the model of adoption to build His church. Since He has specifically put His choice upon us and decided to "grace us" with the same benefits as His "only begotten" Son, doesn't that word picture teach us some profound things about the ministry of adoption of orphan children? My personal understanding of God's purposes and methods has been stretched and expanded in very practical ways. Gerald Clark's observations from the Word of God will challenge you to the very core of your being.

—Glenn Sparks, ThM, Bible teacher and music minister, Community Bible Church, Cave Junction, Oregon

Gerald's message is one that should be heard in every Bible-believing church. It is a transforming message that will revolutionize the church's role in orphan care. His speech is dynamic, succinct, and very moving. Mr. Clark's teaching is well organized, is scripturally sound, and keeps the audience engaged. This speaker is not to be missed if you have a chance to hear him. Gerald and his wife are well worth inviting to your church.

—Dianne Liskey, domestic engineer

In a world where human life is disrespected through abortion, diseases, and abuse, we commend organizations like the Home for Good Foundation that advocate for orphan children yearning for a loving family, and actively promote their adoption.

—Bishop Efraim M. Tendero, national director,
Philippine Council of Evangelical Churches

The teaching of Biblical Adoption from *Adoption and the Gospel* is already bearing fruit around the world. Nearly three thousand pre-publication copies of this book have already been distributed in the USA, Africa and Asia, where Christian families are now adopting children in their own country and culture. Gerald's missionary service in the Philippine orphanage, coupled with the sound Biblical message so appropriately applied in this Bible study, give us a clear direction for adoption ministry that can ultimately lead to solving the world's orphan crisis.

It was 2006 when Gerald and Maureen Clark helped us to launch an adoption ministry in our church. I recall when Gerald first taught from this Bible study about adoption ministry in one of our church's home groups. Only a few days later, the church received a significant donation designated for adoption ministry. Nearly eight years have elapsed, and the church has never lacked for funds in the adoption ministry account, enabling us to come along side of adopting families to help them make their adoptions successful. To date, twelve children have been adopted and more are on the way!

Responding to our Father's heart for adoption has opened our eyes to a whole new ministry paradigm that no one in our church had ever imagined. It was this new vision that resonated with a pastor visiting our church from Uganda, who was already caring for orphans in his own home. Since sharing the message of Biblical adoption with Pastor Daniel, families in his congregation in Uganda have adopted all the children that were in the church's orphanage. He has also been able to teach and distribute this Bible study at several regional and international conferences in Africa, reaching in excess of a thousand churches, where Christian families are now beginning to adopt. Many leaders in those churches are pleading to have their own copies of this book so they can teach their congregations about adoption ministry. This is a testimony to God's purpose in inspiring the writing of this critically needed study.

What *Adoption and the Gospel* has accomplished is truly unique among all the written material available. I have not found any other that brings together the Gospel, the Fatherhood of God, and the Church's call to rescue orphan children in distress, like this book has accomplished. (Prov. 24:11,12) (Ps. 68:5,6) (James 1:27)
                    —Eric Henderson, Church Adoption Ministry Director

Adoption AND THE Gospel

A Biblical Foundation for Adoption as Ministry

from
The Home for Good Foundation

First published online in the public domain
in 2005

Gerald D. Clark

WESTBOW®
PRESS
A DIVISION OF THOMAS NELSON
& ZONDERVAN

Scripture taken from the *New American Standard Bible* ®, copyright © 1960, 1962, 1963, 1971, 1972, 1973, 1975, 1977, 1995 by The Lockman Foundation. Used by permission. Unless otherwise noted.

Scripture quotations marked (NLT) are taken from the *Holy Bible, New Living Translation,* copyright 1996. Used by permission of Tyndale House Publishers, Inc., Wheaton, Illinois 60189. All rights reserved.

Scripture quotations marked (AB) are taken from *The Amplified Bible,* copyright © 1954, 1958, 1962, 1964, 1965, 1987 by The Lockman Foundation (www.Lockman.org). Used by permission.

Scripture quotations marked (KJV) are taken from the Holy Bible: King James Version. 1995. Oak Harbor, Washington: Logos Research Systems, Inc.

WestBow Press books may be ordered through booksellers or by contacting:

WestBow Press
A Division of Thomas Nelson & Zondervan
1663 Liberty Drive
Bloomington, IN 47403
www.westbowpress.com
1 (866) 928-1240

ISBN: 978-1-4908-5492-2 (sc)
ISBN: 978-1-4908-5494-6 (hc)
ISBN: 978-1-4908-5493-9 (e)

Library of Congress Control Number: 2014917940

Printed in the United States of America.

WestBow Press rev. date: 10/08/2014

Contents

Chapter 7

Introduction

For six years, my wife and I participated in the work at a mission orphanage in the Philippines. We gave the children lots of attention and affection and did everything we could to love them, care for them, encourage them, and improve their living conditions. Sometimes, we even brought them to our home for extended stays, but we *always returned them to the orphanage.* We told the children we loved them, but leaving them behind in the orphanage left them wondering. We gave the children everything except our hearts, our home, and our name. We fulfilled their physical needs but never succeeded in giving them a sense of belonging.

For a long time, the children were eager to greet me, and they competed for my attention every time I arrived at the orphanage. I had such joyful times with them, but I always left them behind in the orphanage. No matter how much love and attention I gave them, they were still orphans. If you have ever visited an orphanage, you can probably recall a vivid image of all the children with their happy, smiling faces, frozen in time and never growing older. Your picture of an orphan is exactly what the children want it to be, because it's what they desperately hope will cause you to fall in love with them and take them into your heart, your home, and your life. They are wooing you with every ounce of enthusiasm they can muster. They are so extremely skillful at putting on this façade that I was convinced they were content and happy in the orphanage, and their façade accomplished the exact opposite of what they hoped it would. They not only put on the façade for visitors; they also did it for orphanage staff and administrators! I became an orphanage administrator, and it was a very long time before the façade came down and I was able to observe behavior that demonstrated the children's true feelings.

I had the privilege of meeting two young ladies who were ministering to orphans while living full-time with them in an orphanage. They were volunteers and not orphanage staff and were free to devote all their time and attention to the children who were obviously enjoying this unique relationship. I had instructed them before going on this extended mission to take note of any differences in the behavior of the children based on the presence or absence of orphanage staff and visitors. Both of them reported observing incredible differences in the children's façade or natural behavior. Their reports strongly confirm my own conclusions about the children's façade, after years of pondering their body language and repeatedly asking myself, "What's wrong with this picture?"

When the children finally decided I was never going to adopt them, their behavior began to change and unmask their true feelings, but I still wasn't *getting it*. I was so strongly focused on caring for "orphans" who belong in an orphanage that I couldn't think about caring for "children" who belong in a family. I was too blinded by their façade to understand it. Now I can fully understand why God instructed me when we first arrived in the Philippines that we would be there for six years. I know without any doubt that God had broken my heart for orphans in order to prepare me to devote the rest of my life to adoption ministry.

This study will discuss why orphan ministry is more than just caring for children in an institutional environment (orphanages and foster homes). Orphan care and adoption are equally important means of providing for the care and protection of orphan children, and they both deserve our prayers and financial support. Not all are adoptable, but children belong in families, and every child needs a sense of belonging.

Adoption, as a ministry in the church, is truly a global movement of the Holy Spirit. Unfortunately, adoption currently represents less than 1 percent of ministry to orphan children, but the potential is so much greater! The Holy Spirit has already called countless families to adopt and it just makes sense to match them with children who desperately want to belong to a family. Jesus Himself said, "I will not leave you as orphans ..." (John 14:18) We, and many others, have observed that up to 5 percent of families in churches around the world already have a desire to adopt, which amounts to millions of families. Most of them have never pursued adoption because they assume they could never afford it, and this vast potential remains virtually untapped. Questions that beg to be answered include "What would the Lord have us do?" and "How do we develop a more balanced approach to institutional care and adoption?" Woven throughout this study are suggested ways that anyone can help. For example, pastors can begin by teaching about the biblical doctrine and gospel nature of adoption. They can also share how it relates to evangelizing orphan children and how adoption ministry can empower families to adopt.

I believe that most of the adoptable children in the world could be adopted, by simply identifying and empowering families in our own churches and communities who already want to adopt. This could create a vast amount of vacant orphanage space that is sufficient to care for countless more children who are currently living and dying on the streets.

If you are wondering why ministry to widows and orphans needs to be added to the mission strategy of your church, this study will offer answers from God's Word. Applying James 1:27 to your church's mission strategy can lead to healthy church growth (Matt. 5:16; Job 29:12–13). We should be grateful for those who minister to children in an institutional setting, but we also need to understand the importance of including adoption in every orphan ministry. We need to seek a more balanced approach to orphan ministry by investing far more energy and resources in adoption. We also need to understand that adoption of children by families in their own country and culture is generally far more cost-effective than institutional care.

This study includes statements and documented statistics that may seem unreasonable or exaggerated, but they are all based on observation and personal experience. They have all been confirmed by biblical truth, published statistics, and numerous other adoption and social welfare professionals who have shared similar experiences. I have also sought out and interviewed adult orphans who were never adopted, which further strengthens my resolve to advocate for orphan care and adoption as a dedicated ministry of the church.

God has provided the solution through the beauty and simplicity of adoption ministry. He is calling the church to reestablish its ministry to orphans and widows, and He promises to abundantly bless the people, churches, and nations who heed that call (Deut. 14:28–29; 28:1–2; Mark 9:37). Rather than be overwhelmed with guilt and paralyzed to act, I pray that you will be inspired to participate in this incredible solution that will ultimately help millions of orphan children who so desperately need and want to belong to a loving family. Families who are called to adopt deserve all the help we can give them, and they should not be forced to beg for it. The church is called to be a voice for the children who have no voice, and we need to make it commonly known that help is available through the church (Prov. 31:8–9; Matt. 5:16; 10:8).

Ask God how He wants you to participate in rescuing orphans. He will speak to you through His precious Word and the gentle calling of the Holy Spirit, if you open your heart to hear and obey.

Acknowledgments

This study is dedicated to the children in the various orphanages where I worked or visited, who so persistently, yet painfully, taught me the hard lessons that took me far too long to learn. God knows each of your names, and I pray that they are all written in His Book of Life, especially the ones who slipped through the cracks and vanished into oblivion. I pray they have not fallen victim to child traffickers and predators.

To all the families who have adopted the children that we have shared some small part in helping you accomplish. Your sacrifices and godly examples have been, and continue to be, a huge inspiration to me as I observe the fruit of our shared labors in the lives of the children you adopted.

To our former pastor, Jon Peterson, who challenged me with this question: "What would you do for God's kingdom if cost were no object?" We accepted that challenge, and the result is so aptly stated in Ephesians 3:20–21. "Now to Him who is able to do far more abundantly beyond all that we ask or think, according to the power that works within us, to Him be the glory in the church and in Christ Jesus to all generations forever and ever." Amen.

Most importantly, this book is dedicated to Jesus Christ, who paid such an extravagant price to give me a sense of value and self-worth and paid for my adoption. Thank You for the gift of observation that enabled me to notice the children's behavior that led me to begin asking, "What's wrong with this picture?" Thank You for the ability to understand the spiritual lessons and for the gift of discernment of the Scriptures that inspired me to write this study.

Chapter 1

The Foundation

A Prayer and Scripture to Begin Your Study

Father God, sovereign Lord, thank You that Your spirit is upon me. Thank You that You have anointed me to bring good

> *The Spirit of the Lord God is upon me, because the Lord has anointed me to bring good news to the afflicted.*
>
> —*Isa. 61:1–3*

news to the afflicted, especially orphan children. You have sent me to comfort brokenhearted orphans and tell orphans who mourn that the time of Your favor has come. To orphans who mourn for love and family, You will give beauty for ashes, joy instead of mourning, and praise instead of despair. Thank You, Father, that You adopted me. Let me magnify Your name by bringing more orphan children into Your family. Help me to demonstrate Your love for them by following Your example of adoption and Jesus' example of paying my debt to make my adoption possible.

The Need for an Adoption Bible Study

Not much, if anything, even among already established adoption and orphan ministries, has been written on the theology behind, ministry of, and strategy to implement a ministry of physical adoption. What's more, it is a doctrine that has seldom been practically applied and manifested in the church. (See appendix C.)

Vicar Mark Stibbe wrote, "The doctrine of adoption has been neglected for nearly two thousand years of church history."[1] R. Albert Mohler Jr., president of the Southern Baptist Theological Seminary, asked, "How could the church have been missing this for so long?"[2] Several metaphors, including adoption, are used in the Bible to describe the gospel, and the gospel is incomplete if it fails to include all of them. Adoption needs to be returned to its rightful place in our doctrine and our religion.

I pray this study will serve as a significant contribution toward correcting this long-standing deficiency in the Christian library. Adoption is God's heart for orphans, and I hope that you will come to understand the full richness of the biblical doctrine and gospel of spiritual adoption. We will study adoption as it relates to orphan ministry and how caring for orphans is truly pleasing and honoring to God. We will also discuss how adoption is an excellent way to fulfill the spirit of numerous Scriptures as they apply to orphan children and their needs. It is perhaps one of the best ways to help them become children of God. I hope you will gain a deep appreciation for the practical and evangelistic value of adoption as a ministry, because bringing orphan children into an earthly family and into Gods' family is the ultimate goal of adoption ministry.

There are no explicit commands in the Bible to adopt. However, many Scriptures command us to rescue orphans, care for orphans, fulfill their needs, and defend and plead the cause of orphans. There is a complete list of Scriptures in appendix G. Love is its own mandate, and what better way to truly show our love than through adoption? Caring for children in a permanent family setting is the most likely way to fulfill their deep need for belonging.

The way we respond to the orphan's cry for love reveals the condition of our heart, our love for God, and the depth of our love and appreciation for Jesus Christ, who died to make it possible for us to become children of God. Not all are called to adopt, but anyone can love and minister to orphan children in a very practical and meaningful way, by helping other families adopt. Adoption ministry is about helping families we already know, in our own home church and community, who are called by God and already want to adopt.

God calls all believers to participate in making disciples of all the nations and to help fulfill the needs of others, especially orphans and widows (Matt. 28:18–19; John. 21:15; Gal. 6:2; James 1:27). We can minister to orphans in many ways that seek to fulfill immediate material needs for food, clothing, and shelter. We can also seek to fulfill social, emotional, intellectual, and above all, spiritual needs. However, we must never lose sight of the fact that adoption into God's family is His way of fulfilling our deepest spiritual needs.

Jesus' death on the cross not only atoned for our sins; it also paid for our redemption and spiritual adoption (Rom. 8:23; Gal. 4:4–5) and set another example for us to follow. Many Christian families long to adopt but need a financial miracle to make adoption affordable. Others simply need to understand what the Bible has to say about adoption. Helping families adopt emulates Jesus' example of redemption and should be an integral part of a church's orphan ministry.

Orphan care and adoption ministry belong in the church, and it is my prayer that God's people everywhere will become better informed about adoption. We need to eagerly respond and follow God's example to love and care for orphan children His way (Ps. 68:6). I pray that you will be better equipped to share the good news regarding spiritual adoption and that you will be ready and eager to teach others about God's heart for orphans. Most people don't understand the urgent need for all children to belong to a loving family, and God is calling the church to become their champion.

This study is not intended to be an exhaustive comparison of various forms of orphan care; it is limited to the discussion of spiritual and legal adoption and the children who are adoptable. A great number of children in institutions are not adoptable and will never be adopted. Loving and caring for all institutionalized children is a vital ministry, and for many, it's the first step on the path to adoption. Without this first step, children cannot be adopted! Let's be sure we give the children every possible opportunity to be adopted or to be returned to their family or relatives, whenever possible.

Many children have encountered abuse or abandonment and are already at risk before they ever come to an orphanage or foster home. They are prone to feeling unloved and unwanted and can't understand why God would allow this to happen to them in the first place. It's easy for them to blame God and hard to believe that He loves them. They are scared, vulnerable, lonely, and desperate to be loved and to belong. Some will respond to the love and care they receive in an institutional setting, while many others will be haunted by unanswered questions, such as these: "What's wrong with *me?*" "If God loves me, why am I an orphan?" "If you love me, why don't you adopt me?"

For these children, no amount of love, attention, or care in an institution will substitute for their hunger to belong to a family of their own. Should we blame orphanage staff and supporters? Should we condemn orphan sponsorship because these children don't respond to tender, loving care? Of course not! Instead, we need to recognize that many of these children have been forced into circumstances where it is simply impossible for them to cope or to succeed. Their hearts and emotions have been so badly damaged that without a sense of belonging, they simply are not able or willing to trust or believe anyone. All they know is that they are still orphans.

Consider the example of a taxi driver I met in Manila who told me that he had grown up as an orphan and was never adopted. He was married with two daughters in college. I was delighted to hear that he was so successful, but I was stunned when I inquired about his life in the orphanage and the other children there. He told me that all his peers in the orphanage had become involved in drugs, prostitution, or other criminal activities, and were all dead. He was the only living survivor. I couldn't help but ask why he survived, and he told me it was because of the nuns who came to share their love with him in the orphanage. How could this be? Did the nuns ignore all the other children?

Surely, his friends experienced the same visits from the nuns and all the others who ministered to the children in this orphanage over the years. Why did only one of them survive? Why did only one respond to the love and the affection that was offered? Why did all the others self-destruct? This Bible study seeks to guide us through these and other questions and offer hope as only God's Word can.

Just because we encounter less than perfect success does not mean we should stop trying to do all we can to help the children in every way possible. Not all children can be or will be adopted, and we must continue to love, nurture, and protect them as much as we can. Orphanage staff and caregivers must make every effort to bond with the children and treat them like family, but even that may not be enough.

I spent five days visiting an orphanage and really enjoyed the family atmosphere there. It appeared to me to be as close to perfect as an orphanage could possibly be. It was heavenly and quite a contrast from many other orphanages I have visited or read about. I observed behavior there that one would only expect to see in a very loving family or group of close friends. If that were really true, how can I explain what happened when it was time for me to leave? Four children, varying in age from about eight to eighteen, came to say good-bye and handed me little love notes that were so precious to read, and forced me to choke back the tears. All were handwritten, and two of them were quite lengthy and detailed. What struck me the most is that all four of them specifically asked me to adopt them.

But that does not mean we should summarily condemn orphanages. I could not state it any better than to share what Doug Nichols, of Action International Ministries, wrote in an e-mail dated March 26, 2009. He said,

> Although placing a child into a loving family should be our goal, it is not always possible. God-centered orphanages could bring glory to God and save thousands of children the pain and abuse they face every day on the street. We need to support both adoption and orphanages. So, why shouldn't the church of Jesus Christ start many more orphanages around the world to place street and underprivileged children and orphans into a loving, Christian environment? Orphanages can be safe harbors where children can be lovingly protected and cared for until a home can be found.

Orphanages and foster homes have come to be accepted by many as an end in themselves, rather than as necessary steps on the path toward giving children a loving family and a home for good. Consider this statement by a government official in Africa in March 2009: "We don't want any more orphanages in our country; the outcome for the orphan is not good ... We want the children in families." An application to start a new orphanage in the Philippines was denied, citing the fact that new orphanages are not the desired solution. An orphanage should serve as a transitional home where everything possible is done to achieve a permanent solution for children by returning them to family or relatives, or by accomplishing their adoption.

I have personally witnessed orphan children who displayed clear evidence of being an impossible case for adoption; they were so introverted and so unhappy in the orphanage that I could never make friends with them. Yet when adopted, they made such a miraculous turnaround that if I had not witnessed it myself, I would have found it hard to believe. I'm convinced that we must do everything we can to give the children a sense of permanence and belonging that seems to be possible only in a lifelong, committed relationship that communicates to a child, "I will never abandon or reject you."

I recall a situation with a very troubled girl who had been badly abused, which resulted in her being placed in foster care. Because of her terrible behavior, she had been repeatedly bounced from one foster home to another until a Christian family finally adopted her. Her behavior in her new family was hardly any different, but what made the difference in her life was convincing her that she was finally "home for good." In one of her usual tantrums, she blurted out, "One of these days, I'm going to do something so bad that you're going to throw me out just like everybody else did!" Her daddy took her in his arms and gently, but firmly, told her, "Honey, you've already done those terrible things, several times, and guess what, you're still here! We didn't throw you out. We love you, and we want you to stay with us." He told me that he could almost see the light coming on in her eyes as she came to the realization that what he was telling her was true. She had experienced it being acted out by her new parents. Actions speak louder than words (1 John 3:18)! He told me that her behavior changed overnight, as she was finally able to trust someone, perhaps for the first time in her life.

Without a loving family and the sense of belonging it provides, many orphan children are simply unable to comprehend that anyone could possibly love them. For many orphans, adoption is what it will take to convince them they are loved.

The majority of orphan and foster care delivery systems do not provide for children beyond age eighteen, and many who age out of the system or are "emancipated," as it is often called, are woefully unprepared for life. When I asked an eighteen-year-old orphan boy if he would like to have a family, he told me he wasn't sure, because he didn't know what a family was. Young people like him enter a harsh and unforgiving world with no safety net. He had no employable skills and didn't even know that it was normal and necessary for him to work to support himself.

According to Steven Curtis Chapman, "Statistics regarding the future prospects for children who emancipate from orphanages or the foster care system are profoundly bleak. Ironically, the statistics for American children are almost identical to those for children around the world. Theft, prostitution, homelessness, substance abuse, incarceration, and suicide affect the lives of the vast majority of children who grow up as orphans and never find permanent, loving homes."[3] Neil Bernstein said, "Children raised by the state are disproportionately likely to become homeless, go to jail, have (illegitimate) children as teenagers ..." [4] Also, Vicar Mark Stibbe reported, "Children who spend long periods in institutional care are fifty times more likely to end up in prison than those who don't."[5]

Upon aging out of institutional care, many young people are easy targets for predators and become victims of human trafficking. [6] The director of a well-known Christian adoption agency told me he has repeatedly witnessed predators at orphanages who are already armed with the names of girls and the dates they are scheduled to be released from the orphanage. A pastor told me that while visiting an orphanage in Eastern Europe, he personally witnessed a group of several men dressed in fancy suits arriving in two black limousines. After a brief visit, they kissed the orphanage director and quickly escorted a strikingly beautiful teenage orphan girl into one of their cars and sped away. It is estimated that each year, as many as a half million young girls go directly from an orphanage into the hands of predators who use them for evil intent. Every adoption takes another vulnerable child farther away from this kind of fate.

I pray that these tragic truths will not overwhelm you with guilt but rather will make you keenly aware of an orphan child's desperate need to belong to a family. I hope that you will be motivated to do something to help. A good way to do that is to help families you already know, who need your assistance to make adoption a reality.

Institutional care is the first step toward meeting the needs of orphan children. Adoption is yet another step. A friend stated it this way: "I have come to realize that my volunteering and trying to love and share Christ's love with the children at the orphanage is like putting a bandage on their real problem. The best solution for any of these children is to belong to a family."

When orphans self-destruct, it's not because God doesn't love them. It often happens because they feel unloved and unwanted. How can this be when so many people have given so sacrificially to love, care for, and support these children in an orphanage or foster home? I believe the answer lies not in the quality of the care we give them but rather in how the children perceive our care. No matter how much we love and care for the children, they are still orphans. The problem is not that we fail to care for orphans; the problem is that we simply don't understand that children just don't want to be orphans, and we don't understand their deep need to belong to a family. We've also never heard what happens to most children who remain as orphans.

Jesus tells us in John 14:18, "I will not leave you as orphans." It's interesting to note that the King James Version translates the Greek word *orphanos* as "comfortless." *The Amplified Bible* uses the word *orphans* but amplifies it to mean "comfortless, desolate, bereaved, forlorn, and helpless."

When I heard a young orphan child ask, "If Jesus loves me, why do I have no family?" suddenly the word *comfortless* seemed to make sense. It finally dawned on me why it's so hard for orphans to comprehend God's love and so easy for them to doubt and wonder, "If God loves me, why am I an orphan?" I believe their conclusions result from feeling that they don't belong to anyone. God created us for belonging and placed it in our DNA. Then He said of Adam, "It is not good for the man to be alone," so He created the family to fulfill our need for belonging (Gen. 2:18). Family and belonging are vital elements for emotional well-being, as well as for comprehending God's love. Psalm 68:6 says, "God places the lonely in families" (KJV, NLT AB). Adoption creates belonging and demonstrates love in action. God chose adoption to demonstrate His love for mankind, and I believe that's why so many orphans instinctively long for a family (Gal. 4:4–5; John 1:12; Eph. 1:5). God made us that way.

In the Lord's Prayer, we recite, "Thy will be done, in earth as it is in heaven" (Matt. 6:10 KJV). Jesus said, "I will not leave you as orphans" (John 14:18). Doing God's will on earth as it is in heaven means following His example. Adoption of orphan children models what God has done for us in heaven. Helping other families through their adoption journey, even helping pay for their adoption expenses, models what Jesus Christ did for us on the cross. His blood paid for our adoption into God's family.

Christian families who adopt are missionaries who bring the gospel and God's love to orphan children by living example, making it so much easier for the children they adopt to comprehend God's love and to understand the message of salvation in Galatians 4:4–5 and John 1:12. Regardless of whether we view adoption as ministry or simply a way to build a family, adoption by a Christian family provides a remarkable environment for a child to comprehend God's love, providing the fertile soil where the gospel can take root and thrive (Matt. 13:23).

Many Christian families are eager to adopt, and Romans 10:15 tells us that missionaries must be sent to proclaim the gospel. Can't we say, therefore, that it's biblical to commission, support, and send Christian families as missionaries to bring the gospel to orphan children? (Matt. 10:10). Helping other families adopt is not just a good thing to do; it emulates Jesus' example of redemption. And it can literally be a matter of spiritual life or death for many children who may never have a better chance to discover how much God loves them.

> God is looking for people through whom
> He can do the impossible.
> What a pity we plan to do only the things we can do by ourselves!
> —A. W. Tozer

Why don't you ask God what He wants to do through you? Through your church?

Chapter 1 Reflections

1. Fully understanding our Father's love for us is a key factor in understanding why there is such a longing in our hearts. If you have a copy of *The Father's Love Letter* DVD, this is an appropriate time to view it. The full text of *The Father's Love Letter* is printed in the appendix of this study and is also available in numerous languages from its website: http://www.fathersloveletter.com/.

2. After reading or hearing *The Father's Love Letter*, be sure to read and discuss appendix B, "How to Become an Adopted Child of God." Does this help set a biblical foundation for what we are discussing?

3. We heard some tough words in this chapter. "If God loves me, why am I an orphan?" We usually cannot satisfactorily answer this question, especially if it comes from a child. It may never be verbalized but instead is manifest in a child's behavior. This is a thought for discussion, perhaps not for answers.

4. How do orphan care and adoption relate to the great commission? Does adoption belong as a ministry in the church, or should the government handle it?

5. Discuss John 14:18, Galatians 4:4–5, and John 1:12 and how they relate to each other.

Chapter 2

The Gospel, Doctrine, and Theology of Adoption

A Prayer and Scripture to Begin Your Study

> For the gifts and the calling of God are irrevocable.
>
> —Rom. 11:29

Lord, thank You that You have not left me as an orphan. Show me what my response to the world's orphan crisis should be.

Let's begin our study by ensuring that everyone understands three commonly used words. The word *doctrine* refers to teaching, while the word *gospel* simply means good news, and specifically, the good news that Jesus died for our sins and that He rose again on the third day. Jesus not only died on the cross for our sins and paid for our salvation; He also made it possible for us to become children of God, by way of adoption. I use the word *Christian* to describe any person or church that believes in and abides by the teachings of Jesus Christ, as revealed in His life and death, and in His written Word, the Bible. What we are called or where we attend a church meeting does not make us a Christian. It is who we believe and what we do that makes one a Christian (Rom. 10:9–10). We become a Christian by being adopted into the family of Christ. (John 1:12).

The Bible says in Galatians 4:4–5, "But when the fullness of the time came, God sent forth His Son, born of a woman, born under the law (in subjection to the law), so that He might redeem those who were under the law, (slaves to the law) that we might receive the adoption as sons." In John 1:12, we read, "But as many as received

Him, to them He gave the right to become children of God." Simply stated, God sent Jesus into the world to arrange for our adoption!

We have all heard sermons about having a personal relationship with Jesus Christ, and adoption is the act that creates that personal relationship. Since adoption is the end result of redemption, adoption then is synonymous with salvation. Perhaps now you can understand why Vicar Mark Stibbe says that adoption is one of the ten major doctrines of the Bible.[7] Crucifixion, resurrection, redemption, forgiveness, salvation, justification, born again, eternal life, etc. are all important components of the gospel message of God's love. They all result in the amazing blessing in Galatians 4:5: "that we might receive the adoption as sons." Our adoption into God's family is the ultimate expression of His love and was the ultimate purpose of Jesus' life on earth and death on the cross. Pastor John Piper says it even more strongly, that adoption is the ultimate purpose of the entire universe![8a] He also says, "Galatians 4:4–7 is as central a gospel statement as there is."[8B]

With His blood, Jesus ransomed us from slavery to the law, to make our adoption possible. According to J. I. Packer, "Adoption is the highest blessing of the gospel."[9] Adoption is as much a part of "the gospel" as any other metaphor that is used to describe it. Dr. Russell Moore, former dean of the school of theology at the Southern Baptist Theological Seminary, wrote, "Adoption is about an entire culture within our churches, a culture that sees adoption as part of our great commission mandate and as a sign of the gospel itself."[10]

According to Ken Fong, adoption is an "oft-overlooked biblical metaphor for salvation."[11] This study is intended to help you understand and appreciate that adoption is an integral part of the gospel, and that the gospel is incomplete if it fails to include the doctrine of adoption. Children who are adopted can readily relate to the gospel when it is presented in the context of adoption as stated in Galatians 4:4–5 and John 1:12, and further amplified in Romans 3:23, 6:23, 8:15–23, and 10:9–10.

God chose adoption to demonstrate His love, and Romans 8:15 tells us that we have received "the spirit of adoption as sons," by which we shout to God, "Abba" (most closely translated "Daddy" or "Papa"). From *Easton's Bible Dictionary*, *Abba* is a term of endearment used by children who are totally confident they are cherished and adored by their father. Because of abuse or abandonment by their father, many orphans struggle with a distorted image of a harsh God. Jesus tells us, "Whoever does not receive the kingdom of God like a child will not enter it at all" (Mark 10:15). This verse is not just for orphans; it's for all of us. God wants everyone to relate to Him like a little child with an adoring daddy. Adoption gives orphan children a daddy who can help rebuild their trust in God as a perfect Father. Dr. Russell Moore also describes the Abba cry as a primal scream of terror or panic[12] from a child screaming for the daddy he knows and trusts, because he is confident that his daddy is able to rescue him from whatever threat is terrorizing him or her.

Adoption and Redemption

In Romans 8:23 and Galatians 4:5, the words *redeem* and *redemption* are directly related to adoption. In fact, they are inseparable. Simply stated, God's redemption results in our adoption.

Romans 8:23 says, "And not only this, but also we ourselves, having the first fruits of the Spirit, even we ourselves groan within ourselves, waiting eagerly for our adoption as sons, the redemption of our body." Jesus promised that He would not leave us as orphans in John 14:18. He also tells us in John 14:2–3, "I go to prepare a place for you … and I will come again to (adopt) receive you to myself, that where I am, there you may be also." Love, commitment, permanence, security, face-to-face relationship, and adoption are all unspoken sentiments, assurances, and promises included in these verses. These are some of the many ways that Jesus communicates His love for us, all in the context of adoption.

It's interesting to consider the parallel found in our culture. When a family adopts a child, there are many legal matters to accomplish, both in paperwork and court appearances. This is when the child's redemption from orphanhood actually takes place. Often, a family needs to add a room onto their house to accommodate their new child. In most cases, the child is still in the orphanage, even though everything else is complete. The family must still travel to the orphanage to physically fetch (redeem) their child. This is the day the orphan child has been longing for! For us, as Christians, this is the day when our adoption becomes truly final, the day we leave this earth to go home for good—to join our permanent family, where we meet God, our Abba Father, face-to-face.

By examining every occurrence of the word *redeem* or *redemption* in the Bible, the original Greek or Hebrew means "to release or rescue from loss by the payment of ransom." *Redeem* means to pay whatever debt is owed in order to buy back whatever had been lost, stolen, or forced to be sold. Redemption, in the biblical context, means to restore a person to his or her original status and position in a family. God restores us to His family by means of adoption and gives us a name, a sense of belonging, and full rights of inheritance. Legal adoption of an orphan child is an earthly model that fully emulates God's plan of redemption and spiritual adoption.

The Kinsman Redeemer

Let's look at some biblical examples of redemption. Leviticus 25:25 explains the kinsman redeemer who restored land ownership to its original owner. The Hebrew word for redeem includes "to act as a kinsman" (a close relative such as "next of kin") as part of its definition. The concept of a kinsman redeemer gives us a deep understanding of our redemption and adoption by our heavenly Father. Jesus is our kinsman redeemer.

In the book of Ruth, Naomi and Ruth were both widows with no sons, and thus no inheritance. With no son, Naomi was required by law to sell the land owned by her deceased husband, and with no husband, Ruth would inherit no land. Boaz became the kinsman redeemer who restored land ownership to the family of Naomi's deceased husband. Full payment of debt to redeem the land required Boaz to also take Ruth as his wife because, as Naomi's daughter in law, Ruth was now Boaz' relative. The Bible points out that Boaz was thoroughly delighted with this requirement to marry a beautiful, young woman. This act of redemption returned Naomi and Ruth to their original status in the family, giving Naomi the justice due her and giving Ruth a son with full rights of inheritance of the land of Naomi's deceased husband. As a result of this redemption and inheritance, both Ruth and her son, Obed, became ancestors of King David and Jesus! The right of inheritance is incredibly important to God and is an equally important aspect of family membership that helps to create a sense of belonging. Legal adoption conveys this full right of inheritance to a former orphan child.

The book of Ruth is a beautiful picture of God's plan of redemption and adoption, by restoring the widow and the orphan to their original family. This is an example of what Jesus Christ has done for us by paying for our redemption to restore us to God's family and to restore our inheritance as His fellow heirs (Rom. 8:14–17).

We are all born in sin, separated from God, *illegitimate children, and not sons* (Heb. 12:8). We are spiritual orphans, but Jesus is our kinsman redeemer who offers to restore us to our original status as children of God, and He has already paid the debt of sin that we owed. We have already discovered in Romans 8:23 and Galatians 4:4–5 that redemption results in adoption. The words *redeem* or *redemption* appear over four hundred times in the Bible, indicating that adoption is an important doctrine that is woven throughout the entire Bible. This leaves no doubt that children belong in a family and gives us a godly model to follow.

Theology of the Word *Adoption*

Without theology, adoption is little more than charity. Without mission, it is simply social welfare. Adoption says something about the gospel and God's perfect love that no other word can say! *Salvation* and *redemption* are words that imply "from." (See appendix C) We are saved or redeemed *from* sin and *from* condemnation, but these words alone don't convey the concept of being saved or redeemed *to* anything or anyone. That's why the gospel is incomplete if it fails to include the concept of "to" that is so beautifully communicated in the word *adoption*. We are adopted into a family, ultimately into God's family! Adoption results in a personal, committed, and permanent relationship with God Himself!

Salvation is a wonderful, free gift from God, but without relationship, there is no sense of belonging, and belonging is one of the very highest of human needs. In a relationship, we enjoy much more than simply knowing *about* God; we can actually *know* God. The original Hebrew word for *know* carries the concept of the greatest possible depth of intimacy. God created us for intimacy with Him, and He gave us a glimpse of that intimacy in the marriage relationship. It's no coincidence that the expression *the bride of Christ* is used to describe those who truly *know* God. It's all about an intimate relationship with the Creator of the universe, and it's spoken to us in the words *marriage* and *adoption.*

We choose someone to marry because we have learned from joyful experience that they already have attributes and qualities that are desirable, valuable, and very attractive to us. We are confident we will gain much from an intimate relationship with this person, and these are the things that have caused us to grow into a loving relationship that feels comfortable and safe. The Greek words that describe this kind of love relationship are *storge* and *eros,* "familial love" and "erotic love." Both of these words imply mutual benefit to the ones who love and mutual gratification of our selfish nature.

In addition to creating a legal relationship, marriage is rightfully recognized to be so sacred that the wedding ceremony is usually conducted in a church and pronounced to be blessed by God. It is also blessed by the congregation and celebrated by a large group of friends and relatives.

Adoption is very different, however, and goes beyond choosing someone for all the benefit that one expects to receive from someone they already know and love. Adoption most often involves a conscious decision to choose a child that may have little or nothing to offer. The child may be helpless, and have no skills or abilities, but people still willingly commit to making a great sacrifice to adopt, and to love a child or children regardless of all the unknowns. Only the Greek word *agape* can be used to describe the kind of proactive and sacrificial love that is often demonstrated in adoption! Adoption gives the strongest possible word picture to describe God's agape love for mankind and the incredible sacrifice that Jesus made in order to pay for *our* adoption! Without the concept of agape love that is demonstrated in adoption, the Gospel lacks the full richness it deserves. Adoption is truly one of the richest metaphors we could use for describing the Gospel.

I think it's tragic that we rarely do anything more for adoption than the legal process. In so doing, we continue to neglect the deep spiritual blessing that physical adoption represents, and we fail to celebrate the agape love that it demonstrates. The tragedy continues as we fail to ascribe the same sacredness to adoption that we do to marriage. It's hard to imagine a Christian wedding without a church service, followed by a joyous reception and celebration. We almost never do any of this for adoption! Is it any wonder that many children who have been adopted are ashamed to even be called adopted? Why are we so ashamed to celebrate it? Romans 8:19 describes the final victory celebration where Jesus is proudly introducing His adopted brothers and sisters to all creation. We should be equally proud of our own adoption, and the children we adopt. Without this theological understanding, how can we expect children to be proud of their adoption?

Adoption in Greek, Roman, and Hebrew Culture

Galatians 4:4 begins with "the fullness of the time." This means that God chose a specific time in His story ("history") to reveal His irrevocable, infinite, unconditional love for us in the life and death of His Son Jesus Christ, and to unveil His plan for us to become His children by way of adoption. The fullness of time means, among other things, the precise time chosen by God, which placed Jesus and Paul in the Roman culture so that mankind could fully comprehend Paul's writing about adoption in the context of Roman law, culture, and practice.

Paul was a lawyer, a Roman citizen, and a Pharisee who was highly educated and well acquainted with ancient Greek and Hebrew culture and law. When Paul wrote about adoption in the Bible, he was writing in the context of the existing Roman culture.[13] Why? Although adoption was practiced in Greek culture, if the child did not please the family, he or she could be disowned at any time up to age eighteen. There was no permanent security in a Greek adoption. Adoption did not even exist in Jewish law and was considered unnecessary and, therefore, unknown in Israel. The "seed" or blood connection was vitally important. The concept of adopting someone who was not from the seed of your own family was quite foreign to them.[14] Since the Bible speaks so much and so strongly about caring for widows and orphans, it suggests that throughout history, man has generally failed to give them the care that God desires. Roman law was designed to protect and provide for orphans and most closely demonstrates what the biblical doctrines of election, justification, and sanctification imply.[15]

The Roman culture gives us a living example of the relationship our Abba Father offers to us. The metaphor called "adoption" describes how Jesus shed His blood on the cross to pay our debt of sin in full and make it possible for us to become children of God. In Roman law, adoption was final and irrevocable. A father could disown a biological child, but he could not legally disown a child that he had adopted. Paul used the metaphor of adoption to describe God's great love for us. Like an orphan, God elevated us from a destitute condition to become full members of His royal family. Thus, it was within the context of the Roman culture that God chose to reveal His plan of adoption to us, and represents one segment of the concept of "the fullness of time." This irrevocable aspect of Roman law is a powerful metaphor that communicates the nature of God's unfailing love for the children He has adopted. When a Roman citizen adopted a child, he was required to pay off whatever debts were associated with that child.[16] God redeemed Israel from Egypt. Jesus redeemed us from the debt of sin, and this gives us the model to redeem orphans by helping to pay the cost for their adoption. Whether we adopt a child ourselves or help someone else adopt, we are like the kinsman redeemer who restores an orphan child to a family and gives him or her what they so desperately lack. It blesses us beyond measure and pleases God immensely.

Adoption is a beautiful picture of how God chose us and loved us, even before the foundation of the world, as well as how He sought us when we were not even looking for Him. "He predestined us to adoption as sons through Jesus Christ to Himself, according to the kind intention of His will" (Eph. 1:4–5). This assures us that adoption is not God's second best, and adopted children are not second-rate. Our adoption by God is irrevocable, and this gives us an amazing sense of eternal security (Rom. 11:29).

According to Colossians 1:13–22,

> For He rescued us from the domain of darkness, and transferred us to the kingdom of His beloved Son, in whom we have redemption, the forgiveness of sins. He is the image of the invisible God, the firstborn of all creation. For by Him all things were created, both in the heavens and on earth, visible and invisible, whether thrones or dominions or rulers or authorities-all things have been created through Him and for Him. He is before all things, and in Him, all things hold together. He is also head of the body, the church; and He is the beginning, the firstborn from the dead, so that He Himself will come to have first place in everything. For it was the Father's good pleasure for all the fullness to dwell in Him, and through Him to reconcile all things to Himself, having made peace through the blood of His cross; through Him, I say, whether things on earth or things in heaven. And although you were formerly alienated and hostile in mind, engaged in evil deeds, yet He has now reconciled you in His

fleshly body through death, in order to present you before Him holy and blameless and beyond reproach.

Amazing grace! All of world history can truly be called "His story," because it is the story of what God has done through His Son Jesus Christ, so that we might receive the adoption as sons.

Lessons from the Children

Only three months after arriving in the Philippines, I encountered an incident that shattered my traditional understanding of orphan ministry. This left me seriously disturbed and seeking answers to questions I didn't even know to ask. That's when I began asking myself over and over again, "What's wrong with this picture?"

It was customary for the mission to close the orphanage every Christmas so that each of the children could spend two weeks with a family to experience Christmas in a real home. I could not understand the reaction of an eight-year-old girl when it was time for me to take her back to the orphanage. She had begun to bond with the family that had hosted her, and they told me they wanted to adopt her, but they would not be able to afford the legal fees. "Can't we just keep her?" they asked. I recall thinking, *Wouldn't it be nice if I could just pay the expenses in order to make this adoption possible? It would be even better if there was a ministry for this purpose to help every family who wants to adopt.* Both husband and wife were crying; the girl was crying, and she absolutely did not want to go back to the orphanage.

We explained to her that she could come back to visit again and that the family could come and visit her in the orphanage, but that was just not good enough for her. Though I never used any harsh words or physical force, simply taking her back to the orphanage must have felt like capital punishment to her. A brief glimpse of her dream for a loving family had been wrenched away from her. Her heart was broken and her dream shattered. We had broken her spirit and her despair turned to anger.

Before she met this family, she had been well behaved and reasonably contented, but now she began sneaking out of the orphanage and chasing boys in the local village. Her behavior became so unmanageable that the caregivers could not handle her, so the orphanage director finally had her transferred somewhere else. I have no idea what eventually happened to this girl who vanished into oblivion. Her memory burns forever in my heart and will help fuel my passion for adoption ministry for as long as I live. I was shaken to the very core and "ruined" as Kay Warren calls it. I simply could not understand what was wrong with this picture. But I knew it was terribly wrong. Since that fateful day in January 1997, I have been advocating for adoption as a ministry in every evangelical church in the world.

I was such a novice to orphan ministry at that time that the concept of foster care never entered my mind. For very little investment at all, this family could have become foster parents for this girl, and we could have gone out and raised the money for her adoption. It's even more tragic that the orphanage staff wasn't prepared to offer the foster care option to this family. None of us understood the urgency that this girl so desperately tried to communicate to us.

Chapter 2 Reflections

1. Being adopted by the God of the universe is the greatest blessing that anyone could ever receive. Here are some interesting parallels comparing spiritual adoption to legal adoption of orphan children.

   • Adoption is irrevocable (Rom. 11:29).
   • Adopted children cannot be disowned (Heb. 13:5; Deut. 31:6, 8).
   • Can our heavenly Father disown us?
   • What about our earthly father?

2. The adopted child receives a new family name. Spiritually, we are in the family of God and our family name is "Christian." Many adopted children also receive a new first or given name in addition to a new family name. Revelation 3:12 tells us we receive a new heavenly name too. Why is it important to connect to our family with a first name or given name?

3. Read Revelation 3:5 and 2 Corinthians 5:17. It is traditional for a child who is being adopted by an earthly family to leave all their old clothes behind at the orphanage or foster home. The child is given new clothes that come from the adopting family. Some orphan children can't wait to take off their "orphan clothes" and put on the new garments that identify them with their new family. Can you draw any parallels between this tradition and Revelation 3:5 and 2 Corinthians 5:17?

4. There is a cost involved. Jesus' shed blood was expensive love (John 3:16; Rom. 8:32). Not only is there a cost, but Jesus

was willing to pay that cost no matter how expensive it was. It cost Him everything—every day of His earthly life. Could this apply to the adoption of a child into an earthly family?

5. Most adoptive families have an understanding of this equality of rights between their biological children and those who joined the family via adoption, even if they cannot explain it in biblical terms. God undoubtedly knew their tender hearts for children and gave them a divine understanding and discernment about adoption. Comment on this, but be patient if you are not yet fully equipped to share it or understand it.

Chapter 3

The Family of God and Our Divine Heritage

A Prayer and Scripture to Begin Your Study

Abba, Father! Thank You for allowing me to become Your beloved child. May this knowledge inspire me and may Your love fill me to overflowing so I can be a part of bringing Your gift of adoption to countless orphans who don't yet know You.

> *Who are Israelites, to whom belongs the adoption as sons, and the glory and the covenants and the giving of the Law and the temple service and the promises.*
> —*Rom. 9:4*

By now, we know what it means to be adopted into the family of God. At the same time that we are adopted, we also become sons of Abraham. "And now that you belong to Christ, you are the true children of Abraham. You are his heirs, and now all the promises God gave to him belong to you" (Gal. 3:29 NLT).

This is very comforting to us all, but especially to those who have never known their earthly father or whose father was not loving and kind. Adoption is our spiritual heritage, but what about earthly adoptions? Indeed, there are some stunning examples in the Bible. You may be very familiar with the stories and characters, but rarely are they discussed in the context of adoption. As we look at these stories, you will see that God chose to change the world and to fulfill prophecy by using people who were adopted.

Gerald D. Clark

Moses Was Adopted

The story of Moses' adoption illustrates a form of "salvation" for the nation of Israel and serves as a living parallel to God's plan of redemption through adoption that He revealed to us in the life and death of His Son Jesus. All the male children of the Hebrew slaves in Egypt were condemned to death by decree of Pharaoh, yet Moses' life was supernaturally redeemed (saved) when he was taken in and raised by Pharaoh's own daughter.

Moses' adoption prepared him for a remarkable life. Since he grew up in Pharaoh's household, he was very acquainted with, and not intimidated by, the power of Pharaoh's position. When God sent Moses to demand that Pharaoh let His people (Israel) go, Moses was well equipped for face-to-face confrontation with Pharaoh. Read Exodus 6:28–7:7. At age forty, when he killed an Egyptian for beating an Israelite, Moses was forced to flee for his life and live for forty years in the wilderness. God used this time to prepare Moses for his future assignment of leading Israel out of Egypt, through the Red Sea into the very same wilderness where he would eventually spend another forty years before reaching the Promised Land. It was the same wilderness where Moses first met God in the burning bush on Mount Sinai. After leading Israel out of Egypt, Moses again met God on the same mountain, when he received the Ten Commandments.

Bible scholars say that Moses is a "type" of Messiah, because just like Jesus, Moses grew up to become God's instrument of salvation for Israel. The story of Moses' adoption would help Israel recognize their coming Messiah, and Moses referred to that when he prophesied of the coming Messiah. He said in Deuteronomy 18:15–18,

> The LORD your God will raise up for you a prophet like me from among you, from your countrymen, you shall listen to him. This is according to all that you asked of the LORD your

30

God in Horeb on the day of the assembly, saying, "Let me not hear again the voice of the LORD my God, let me not see this great fire anymore, or I will die." The LORD said to me, "They have spoken well. I will raise up a prophet from among their countrymen like you, and I will put My words in his mouth, and he shall speak to them all that I command him."

It's interesting to note that Moses did not lose his biological family identity. Read Exodus 2:5–10. God arranged for Moses' biological mother to become a servant of Pharaoh's daughter so she could nurture her own son. Not long after Moses escaped from Egypt, God sent his brother Aaron to find him in the wilderness. Moses, Aaron, and their sister Miriam lived out the rest of their lives together after leaving Egypt.

Esther Was Adopted

Take a few minutes to read the inspiring book of Esther. You really must see Esther's story in light of this study. Before becoming queen of Persia, Esther's parents died, and verse 2:7 tells us that her cousin, Mordecai, raised Esther as his own daughter. Like Moses, this child of adoption grew up to become God's instrument of salvation for the entire nation of Israel. God truly wants us to understand that people who were adopted play major roles in His plan of salvation. They are not second-class citizens.

The Bible tells us that both Moses and Esther were treated like full members of the family. They were both chosen, not of their own doing, and found themselves in royal families with power and influence that led to their becoming God's instruments of salvation. I believe God intended for us to understand these stories as examples of our own adoption into His royal family, so that we could understand

His plan for us to also become powerful instruments of salvation for people in our world today.

God has placed in our hearts a strong sense of family heritage. We are made in His image and have a natural desire to belong not only to an earthly family but also to God's family. It is this longing that leaves such an empty void in the core of every orphan child that adoption fills so beautifully. Isn't it great to know that no matter what our family circumstances are here on earth, we have a priceless heritage to claim? All the promises God gave to Abraham already belong to us, but even more than that. We are humbled to know that upon our entrance into heaven, we will share equally with Jesus all the blessings of God's kingdom. Romans 8:17 says, "And if children, heirs also, heirs of God and fellow heirs with Christ, if indeed we suffer with Him in order that we may also be glorified with Him." All because we are God's children!

Jesus, the Son of Joseph, the Son of David, the Son of Abraham

In numerous Scriptures, Jesus is called the son of David. Some say this implies that Jesus was adopted by Joseph. In Isaiah 7:14, he prophesied that the Messiah would be born of a virgin. Joseph knew that he was not Jesus' biological father, and by adopting Jesus, Joseph would have given Him the legal right to be called the son of David (Matt. 1:19). Joseph raised Jesus as his own child, and other children in his family are referred to in the Bible as brothers and sisters of Jesus.

Some believe that Mary was also a descendant of King David, but even if she was, in the Hebrew culture, family lineage was transmitted from father to son,[17] and Jesus' ancestry and lineage from

Abraham through King David is clearly traced though Joseph (Matt. 1:1–17; Luke 3:23–31).

Isaiah, Jeremiah, and David all knew that Messiah would be called the "Son of David" as seen in the following Scriptures: Psalm 132:11–18, Isaiah 9:6–7, Isaiah 11:1–5, and Jeremiah 23:5–6. The people who lived in Jesus' time also knew that Messiah would be known as "the Son of David." This is found in Matthew 1:1, 12–23, 21–9, and 22:42–45 and Luke 1:31–32. The genealogy of Jesus establishes a clear line of ancestry, which many believe could only be complete if Jesus was recognized as a legally adopted son of Joseph.

The Bible indicates that Jesus was considered to be a legal member of the family. Regardless of how we define it, Jesus' relationship to Joseph and to King David gives us a picture of adoption that bestows full rights of family lineage and inheritance upon the adoptee. These are the same benefits we receive as children of God.

Beth Moore said this so beautifully in one of her Bible studies many years ago. "Christ's royal lineage would come through His adoptive father (Joseph). We shouldn't be surprised at the profound significance with which God views adoption. God the Father allowed His Son to be adopted into a family on earth so that we could be adopted into His family in Heaven."[18]

Lessons from the Children

One day, while visiting another orphanage, I met a girl who had been born with cerebral palsy and suffered profound hearing loss. She was a very friendly girl with a ready smile and seemed to be totally comfortable with me. I was immediately drawn to her and we became friends quickly. I asked for permission to photograph her and use her story and photos to assist in raising the funds to purchase hearing aids and pay for the associated medical tests. While I went to get my camera, one of the orphanage staff explained to the girl in sign language what was about to take place.

As soon as I got my camera set up, and without any instruction from me, she began to strike poses like a professional model, which resulted in a series of beautiful photos. I was already falling in love with her and couldn't help but wonder why she had been in this orphanage for ten years. Who wouldn't want to adopt such a sweet and friendly girl? I recall thinking, *I could adopt a girl like her,* but I began to grieve in my spirit, knowing there were so many more just like her who were just as lovable, and I was overwhelmed by the magnitude of it all. I didn't even recognize it when she said, "I love you," in sign language, and many months passed before someone finally pointed it out to me in one of the photos. Immediately, my eyes began filling with tears of joy, but I was sad that I had not noticed or appropriately responded to her love.

It was several months before I was able to return to the orphanage with the funds for her hearing aids, and I was excited to be able to see this little sweetheart again and to finally respond appropriately to her expression of love. I was eager to scoop her up in my arms and just hug her as long as she would let me hold her, but I was totally unprepared for what happened next. The moment she saw me, she frowned with obvious disapproval and walked away. I thought perhaps she had forgotten me, so I caught up with her and stooped down to pick her up, but she resisted and ran away. When I tried again, I could tell she really wanted nothing to do with me, and when I asked one of the staff if they would help me reconnect with her, they told me that she didn't want to see me and that I should not make any further attempts. I was heartbroken, but that soon turned to a very sick feeling when I finally realized what had happened.

During the photo session, I had made her feel like a princess. Though I did nothing special, I was giving her an amazing amount of attention. Suddenly, I remembered about her signing, "I love you," and God showed me in that moment how my attention was all it took to give this girl a glimmer of hope that I might be the one to finally adopt her. She was already letting me know that she was willing and eager, and she confirmed it by signing that she loved me, but I was too naïve to figure it out. I didn't recognize how strongly she was wooing me. Instead, I just vanished out of her life, dashed her hopes to death, and shattered her vulnerable heart. I had offended her so badly that it's no wonder she didn't want to see me again.

I'm convinced that I caused this girl to stumble, and now I can understand why so many of the other orphans I worked with displayed similar behavior when I tried to love them. They all carried the same unspoken and unanswered question in their hearts. "If you love me, why don't you adopt me?" My interaction with this girl accomplished the exact opposite of what I intended.

Experiences like these have given me the passion to do whatever it takes to help people understand how difficult it is for a child to feel loved and wanted and how fragile and vulnerable their emotions are, whether they are on the streets or in an orphanage.

Chapter 3 Reflections

1. God chose to prepare us for our adoption and to set the stage for the coming Messiah through the remarkable examples of Moses and Esther leading up to Jesus. There is so much love for us woven into these examples that it is hard to absorb it all. Most have never looked at adoption through this lens. Take time to discuss, and then write your thoughts and prayers.

2. Comment on the picture you now have in your mind of your spiritual adoption in contrast with the way our culture views adoption.

3. Did you know that ancestry searching is one of the fastest-growing hobbies in America? Is it any wonder why, considering our heritage and our deepest needs? Let's reflect on this growing hobby.

4. Is it possible to see that there is an enemy who not only does not want adoption to happen in the earthly sense, but who also does not want us to truly understand the profound significance of our heavenly adoption and our divine heritage? Discuss your thoughts on this.

5. There have been some amazing parallels to adoption found in this study so far. Perhaps it's time to reflect on your new insights.

Chapter 4

Commands, Instructions, Promises, Blessings, and Warnings

A Prayer and Scripture to Begin Your Study

Disturb me from my complacency, oh God. Burn into my heart Your commands and allow it to drive me to action. When the day is over, may I remember to thank You for this divine privilege.

> Lord, You know the hopes of the helpless. Surely You will listen to their cries and comfort them. You will bring justice to the orphans and the oppressed, so people can no longer terrify them.
>
> —Ps. 10:17–18 NLT

God derives great pleasure in using ordinary people to accomplish His purposes and fulfill many of His promises. They are obedient servants who are equipped with the knowledge of His word and His will, and they know what pleases Him. God loves to abundantly bless His faithful children who are prayed up, ready for action, and Spirit led and proactive about doing His will.

James 1:22 tells us to be doers of the word, not merely hearers who deceive ourselves. Verse 25 says, "This man will be blessed in what he does" (emphasis on the doing). James 2:15–17 says that if we don't do something to fulfill the needs that God sets before us, our faith is useless. John 21:15–17 shows us clearly that it is what we do that proves our love for Jesus. He said in John 21:15, "Do you love Me?" "Tend my lambs." He also said in Matthew 25:40, "To the extent that you did it to one of these brothers of mine, even the least of them, you did it to me." All these verses direct us to the *doing* of God's will and work.

Numerous Scriptures tell of God's concern, love, protection, and provision for orphans. We will now examine God's commands, promises, blessings, and warnings regarding orphans and how He has called us individually and corporately, as the church, to be His instruments of blessing to fulfill His promises. We are the provision that God has already supplied to preserve the orphan's life, to defend the orphan, to provide a home, and to show love and mercy to orphans.

Fields of the Fatherless: The Law and Practice of Gleaning

Lev. 19:9–10; 23:22; Deut. 24:19–21

God commanded farmers not to harvest the crops out to the very edges or into the corners of their fields. This strip of land was like a wide border completely surrounding the field, and it was reserved for Levites, aliens, widows, orphans, and the poor and needy who could come and harvest whatever crops were there. This was called gleaning, and gleaners were the only ones allowed to harvest what grew within the borders. Every landowner was required to provide this land as an integral part of God's plan to ensure that His people would always provide for orphans and widows.

These fields eventually came to be known as the fields of the fatherless. In God's mind, as revealed in the following command, this land literally belonged to the fatherless. Proverbs 23:10 commands, "Do not move the ancient boundary or go into the fields of the fatherless." The dividing line between the farmer's field and the fields of the fatherless was called "the ancient boundary." Harvesting in the fields of the fatherless was a sin, unless one was in the named group of gleaners. Apparently, some landowners would actually move the ancient boundary to make their harvest area larger and the fields of the fatherless smaller. This too was a sin, which is specifically prohibited in Proverbs 23:10.

A second command is applied to the farmer's portion of the field. Once the workers had harvested the owner's crops, they were not allowed to return again for any further harvest, even if more crops remained or ripened at a later date. The entire field was required to be left for the gleaners after the first harvest.

The Sacred Portion

Deuteronomy 14:28–29 commands,

At the end of every third year you shall bring out all the tithe of your produce in that year, and shall deposit it in your town. The Levite, because he has no portion or inheritance among you, and the alien, the orphan and the widow who are in your town, shall come and eat and be satisfied, in order that the Lord your God may bless you in all the work of your hand which you do.

To be sure we didn't miss it, God repeated the instruction in Deuteronomy 26:12–13, and for further emphasis, He gave it a special name: "the Sacred Portion." This portion is in addition to the gleaning that was already allowed in the fields of the fatherless. God assigned such high priority to the ministry that He has even established a special, designated funding for it: the sacred portion. Malachi 3:8–9 tells us that Israel was cursed for withholding tithes and offerings. Then, in verse 10, God promised an amazing blessing if His people were obedient to give the full tithe, which I believe includes the sacred portion to feed and care for orphans.

> Bring the whole tithe into the storehouse, so that there may be food in My house, and test Me now in this," says the LORD of hosts, "if I will not open for you the windows of heaven and pour out for you a blessing until it overflows.

In every other area of our lives, we are sternly warned not to test God, but when it comes to giving for ministry, God challenges us to test Him. There is nothing mysterious or cryptic in this command. Obedience would result in overflowing abundance of blessing.

The sacred portion was of such high priority that God wanted Israel to understand that it was not a freewill offering. It was a command for everyone, just like James 1:27 is a command for today's church. Not giving the full tithe is described in Malachi 3:8 as robbing God. James 4:17 makes a similar statement in the New Testament. "Therefore, to one who knows the right thing to do and does not do it, to him it is sin." Jesus makes it clear that the spirit and intent of the sacred portion is still relevant in the church today, when He said,

> I did not come to abolish the law of Moses or the writings of the prophets. No, I came to fulfill them. I assure you, until heaven and earth disappear, even the smallest detail of God's law will remain until its purpose is achieved.
> Matt. 5:17–18 NLT

Under the new covenant, we are not bound to the letter of the law of Moses or the writings of the prophets. But as followers and disciples of Jesus Christ, we are bound by love to fulfill the spirit of the law. The fulfillment of the law and the prophets is defined in Matthew 22:37–40.

You shall love the Lord your God with all your heart, and
with all your soul, and with all your mind. This is the great
and foremost commandment. The second is like it, You shall
love your neighbor as yourself.' On these two commandments
depend the whole Law and the Prophets.

In order to know how to fulfill the spirit of the law regarding
widows and orphans, we must understand God's heart and priority
for these ministries. The description of the sacred portion and the
gleaning in the fields of the fatherless give us an undeniable picture
of God's heart for widows and orphans and His priority for the only
ministries in the Bible that are called pure and undefiled religion.
They are clearly defined, high priority, and intentional.

God is calling His church to minister to widows and orphans
with the same intentional priority. He wants every orphan to be
adopted into His family, and He wants the world to observe the
church practicing pure and undefiled religion.

Other Commands regarding Orphans

Deut. 16:14   "And you shall rejoice in your feast, you and your son
and your daughter and your male and female servants
and the Levite and the stranger and the orphan and the
widow who are in your towns."

Ps. 82:3   "Defend the poor and the fatherless (orphan)" (KJV).

When you look into the original Hebrew, this could also be translated
as "Deliver the poor and the orphan" (from their affliction).

Prov. 3:27   "Do not withhold good from those to whom it is due,
when it is in your power to do it."

Prov. 24: 11,12   "Rescue those who are unjustly sentenced to death; don't stand back and let them die. Don't try to avoid responsibility by saying you didn't know about it. For God knows all hearts, and he sees you. He keeps watch over your soul, and he knows you knew! And he will judge all people according to what they have done." (NLT)

Prov. 31:8–9   "Speak up for those who cannot speak for themselves; ensure justice for those who are perishing. Yes, speak up for the poor and helpless, and see that they get justice" (NLT).

Isa. 1:17   "Learn to do good; Seek justice, Reprove the ruthless, Defend the orphan, Plead for the widow."

Jer. 22:3   "Do not mistreat foreigners, orphans, and widows" (NLT).

Zech. 7:10   "Do not oppress widows, orphans, foreigners, and poor people" (NLT).

Mark 10:14   "Permit the children to come to Me; do not hinder them; for the kingdom of God belongs to such as these."

Instructions to Take Action

Jesus taught His disciples to demonstrate their love for Him by their actions.

John 21:15   "Simon son of John, do you love me? … Tend my lambs."

James 1:22   "But prove yourselves doers of the word, and not merely hearers who delude themselves."

1 John 3:18   "Little children, let us not love with word or with tongue, but in deed and truth."

Dan. 11:32   "People who know their God will display strength and take action."

Ps. 10:14   "You are the defender of orphans" (NLT).

Hosea 14:3   "For in You the orphan finds mercy."

Ps. 68:5–6   "Father to the fatherless, defender of widows … God places the lonely in families" (NLT).

Matt. 25:40   "Truly I say to you, to the extent that you did it to one of these brothers of Mine, even the least of them, you did it to Me."

Mark 9:37   "Anyone who welcomes a little child like this on my behalf welcomes me, and anyone who welcomes me welcomes my Father who sent me" (NLT).

Promises and Blessings

In an ideal world, there would be no sin, no suffering, no poverty, and no orphans. But this is a fallen world; there is sin in it. What if there was an ideal church, even in a fallen world? The Bible clearly states in Deuteronomy 15:4–5 that there would be no poor among us *if* only we would listen obediently to the voice of the Lord our God, to observe carefully, and to obey all His commandments. There might also be far fewer orphans if God's people were carefully obeying His commandments regarding orphans. The words *bless, blessed* or *blessing* are repeated more than forty times in Deuteronomy, because God wants us to know that He truly and very seriously means it. Take special notice of Deuteronomy 14:28–29, where God promises blessings upon those who faithfully provide for orphans (and others). The more we bless and care for orphans and the more we give them of what they really need, the more God will bless us. "But you shall freely open your hand to him, and shall generously lend him sufficient for his need in whatever he lacks" (Deut. 15:8). "Whatever" an orphan lacks surely includes a home and a family.

Read Deuteronomy chapter 28 about God's promises of blessing, especially verses 1 and 2

43

Now it shall be, if you diligently obey the LORD your God, being careful to do all His commandments which I command you today, the LORD your God will set you high above all the nations of the earth. All these blessings will come upon you and overtake you if you obey the LORD your God.

Notice two things about these verses. First, look at the words "careful to do." As we learn in James 1–2, we must be doers of the Word in order to receive the blessings. Second, look at the word "overtake." Blessings will overtake us; we cannot escape them, if only we do what we are commanded to do. This chapter alone repeats variations of the word *bless* ten times.

God considers helping orphans an unblemished act of worship, and He blesses people and nations who are willing to fulfill their needs (James 1:27). When we do so, the Lord will bless us in all the work of our hands (Deut. 14:29). We should take special note whenever God repeats something in His Word. Several such repeated promises of blessing are listed later in this chapter. Loving orphans is the very heart of God. That's why He says, "Anyone who welcomes a little child like this on My behalf welcomes Me" (Mark 9:37 NLT). When we live our lives in a way that reflects the heart of God, He is pleased and promises to bless us.

Blessings upon Those Who Are Generous to the Poor, Widows, and Orphans

Deut. 14:29   "The orphan and the widow who are in your town, shall come and eat and be satisfied, in order that the Lord your God may bless you in all the work of your hand which you do."

Deut. 24:19   "When you reap your harvest in your field and have forgotten a sheaf in the field, you shall not go back to get it; it shall be for the alien, for the orphan, and for the widow, in order that the Lord your God may bless you in all the work of your hands."

Ps. 41:1   "How blessed is he who considers the helpless; The Lord will deliver him in a day of trouble."

Prov. 11:25 "The generous man will be prosperous."

Isa. 58:7–8 (about fasting) "I want you to share your food with the hungry and to welcome poor wanderers into your homes. Give clothes to those who need them, and do not hide from relatives who need your help. If you do these things, your salvation will come like the dawn. Yes, your healing will come quickly. Your godliness will lead you forward, and the glory of the Lord will protect you from behind" (NLT).

Jer. 22:16   "He made sure that justice and help were given to the poor and needy, and everything went well for him. Isn't that what it means to know me?" asks the Lord (NLT).

Warnings

Numerous Scriptures clearly indicate that God is very displeased with those who exploit or oppress orphans. (Isa. 10:2; Zech. 7:10; Mal. 3:5) His strong warnings are easily understood but frequently overlooked. God is calling His church to defend and protect orphans in every way possible that gives her a wealth of opportunities to demonstrate God's love to the entire world (Matt. 5:16). Also included is a warning against doing nothing, or refusing to help. (Isa. 1:23; Jer. 5:28)

True Justice Due Orphans

"Speak up for those who cannot speak for themselves; ensure justice for those who are perishing. Yes, speak up for the poor and helpless, and see that they get justice" (Prov. 31:8–9 NLT).

"You shall not pervert the justice due an alien or an orphan, nor take a widow's garment in pledge" (Deut. 24:17).

"The sure way to deprive orphans of the justice due them is to do nothing.[19] C. Thomas Davis

Doing nothing is actually defined as opposing God. "Anyone who isn't helping me opposes me, and anyone who isn't working with me is actually working against me" (Matt. 12:30 NLT). Doing good works is not what saves us. We are saved by faith alone. But doing good works is the proof that our faith is real. Not only is it real to God, it is also real to orphan children, and the witness of our doing is real to all the world. Adoption then, is an evangelistic witness to orphan children and to all the world (Matt. 5:16).

I believe that true justice due orphans is simply doing for orphans what God has done for us. "Freely you received; freely give" (Matt. 10:8).

Spiritual warfare is real and it is constant (Rom. 7:21–23; Eph. 6:12). The Enemy always works to distort the truth of God's Word. He is the accuser who always tells us we are guilty and worthless. He wants us to feel paralyzed by the orphan crisis, overwhelmed by the message, powerless to act, and guilty for allowing the crisis to exist in the first place. He wants to destroy the family and the hope of a future family for orphans.

There is a Grim Truth When God's People Fail to Act

The Center for Adoption Research reports that the longer a child spends in institutional care, the more emotional trauma they accumulate.[20] This statement, and the statistics regarding negative outcomes that await many orphan children, can hardly be called justice.

It's no surprise that statistics regarding children who grow up in institutional care are so grim. Many have been placed there because they have been abused, neglected, molested, or abandoned. Others have lost loving parents by death, and they can't understand why God would allow that to happen to them. By the time they arrive at an orphanage or foster home, they have probably lost everything they have cherished in life. Their home, family, love, sense of belonging, security, and self-worth are devastated. Their future is totally uncertain and they are really scared. They have no physical or emotional security, and it's difficult or even impossible for them to comprehend God's love and His offer of eternal security. They are easily convinced that God must not love them. Consider the impact of adoption that gives an orphan child a permanent home, a loving family, and a sense of belonging. What a powerful way to demonstrate God's love by living example, and to restore what too often has been unjustly taken from them. Doing nothing serves to perpetuate the injustice.

Lessons from the Children

One young girl had been badly abused before coming to the orphanage. She was terrified of any strange man and would not come near me. I had never met a child with whom I couldn't make friends, until I met this girl. If I moved in her direction, she would quickly run away. If I pursued her, she would scream and cry. She never smiled, rarely played with the other children, and was always by herself. We were very concerned that she would have difficult adjustment issues if she were to be adopted, so we prayed and asked the Lord to send just the right family for her. We made sure that her adoption dossier informed any prospective family of her condition.

When she was matched with a family, we prayed for them to be well prepared, and the Lord answered even beyond our expectations. When they came to redeem her from the orphanage, she would allow her new mother to pick her up but would not go near her father. They were well prepared and executed their plan perfectly. Whenever there was discipline to apply, it came from Mom, but whenever the girl needed or wanted anything, her father was the only one who would respond. Mom deliberately ignored her requests and sent her to Daddy. It wasn't long before she figured it out and learned to deal with it, but it took considerably more time before she was finally comfortable with it. Dad had to work hard to earn her trust, but their plan gave him lots of hands-on opportunities.

Letters from the family assured us that her adjustment was progressing well, but we were guardedly optimistic—well, more like slightly skeptical. Six months later, we were visiting relatives not far from where this family lived so we decided to visit them and see for ourselves. When we arrived, the girl remained aloof, but polite, and did not seem to be fearful, but I stuck with my plan not to get too close and risk upsetting her. When her mother introduced us and asked her daughter if she remembered us, she said that she did.

After dinner, I sat down on the floor in the children's playroom to observe her playing with her new brother, but I remained as far away as possible. After several minutes, she finally noticed me there, stopped, and stared at me for quite some time. I could tell her mind was processing something, but I remained still and only smiled at her from a distance. Then, after a very long pause, she began walking slowly toward me. I froze, but my mind was racing with anticipation of what might happen next. Much to my delight, she came right up to me, wrapped her arms around my neck, and gave me the sweetest hug. And she was okay when I hugged her back! My cup runneth over! And so was hers. For the first time in her life, she had enough love in her heart to give some away.

It was only then that I could begin to understand her emptiness back in the orphanage. Belonging was the missing link. To this day, I still tend to weep tears of joy every time I share this experience.

Chapter 4 Reflections

1. Comment on the commands. What stands out for you?

2. Comment on the promises and blessings. What stands out for you?

3. Could it be that the lengthy time it takes for authorities to accomplish an adoption might also be considered perverting the justice due an orphan and subject to judgment?

4. Read Malachi 3:5. It's a strong warning not mentioned in this chapter.

5. Read Isaiah 10:1–2. These verses make a very strong statement about legal systems and the treatment of orphans. This may raise more questions than answers and may lead to a lively discussion. Discuss your observations with other members in your group, and try to suggest ways that you could be helpful. Is any of this relevant today?

6. Read Isaiah 1:23 and write out a prayer for leaders in your community and country. Read it aloud to your group. Stand on the promises found in 2 Chronicles 7:14. Take the time now to pray for your leaders.

Chapter 5

Fulfilling Our Divine Privilege as Members of the Family of God

A Prayer and Scripture to Begin Your Study

Abba Father, break my heart with the things that break Your heart. Fill my heart with the love that fills Your heart. Fill me with compassion to care and courage to act. Let me become a doer of Your Word with faith to move mountains—better yet, faith to move children from bondage to freedom, from slavery to redemption, and from orphans to heirs!

> *For God is working in you, giving you the desire to obey Him and the power to do what pleases Him.*
> *—Phil. 2:13 NLT*

By now, you may be thinking, *There are so many important things to do for the kingdom of God. How can we do them all?* Remember, God never calls anyone to do them all. Each member of the family of God has different skills, gifts, and responsibilities. Ephesians 4:11 tells us that some are called to be apostles, some prophets, others evangelists, pastors, or teachers. First Corinthians 12 describes spiritual gifts and how God uniquely equips each person to be involved in a specific ministry function. First Corinthians 12:28–30 tells us there are gifts of miracles and healings, the gift of helps, administrations, and various kinds of tongues, but not all are given the same gifts. Just as we are not all called to adopt, the Holy Spirit distributes spiritual gifts and talents according to God's will and plan for each person.

God has a unique plan for each of our lives. "For we are His workmanship, created in Christ Jesus for good works, which God prepared beforehand so that we would walk in them" (Eph. 2:10). He does not ask us to do everything, and there is no guilt in doing only that which we are called to do. He calls each of us to a specific ministry for which He has already gifted and equipped us and He has already preordained a plan for our life that will result in a significant contribution to His kingdom. God often confirms His calling through ordinary people and normal life circumstances, as well as our natural talents and desires. Psalm 37:4 tells us to "delight yourself in the Lord, and He will give you the desires of your heart." "For God is working in you, giving you the desire to obey Him and the power to do what pleases Him" (Phil. 2:13 NLT). When we function within our calling, God blesses us and we are energized and enthusiastic about our work, and we rarely tire of it. The fact that you have a desire to adopt, or have an interest in learning about adoption and ministering to orphans, is a good indicator that God may have called you to this specific ministry. Prayerfully ask Him to confirm His plan for your life. Ask for faith and discernment to follow His plan one day at a time, one prayer at a time.

Many people in ministry encounter incredible resistance, opposition, and persecution. Some see it as evidence of being out of God's will, but consider this: Jesus was never out of God's will, yet He encountered severe opposition, persecution, and even death!

Love is more than just thoughts or feelings. Love is best expressed in action (1 John 3:18). Any activity that claims or intends to be ministry must include a powerful expression of the gospel acted out daily in our lives that inspires others and attracts them to the love of Jesus Christ. Adoption is an example of a powerful expression of the gospel, lived out daily in the life of a former orphan child. That's why we say that Christian families who adopt are missionaries who bring God's love to orphan children by living example. After being adopted, imagine a child maturing in his or her faith and discovering this amazing parallel to his or her spiritual adoption. Imagine other people discovering this same parallel.

Matthew 5:16 says, "Let your light shine (i.e., practice your religion) before men in such a way that they may see your good works, and glorify your Father who is in heaven." Adoption is an excellent example of letting our light shine. When we practice pure and undefiled religion, Jesus is lifted up (glorified, exalted), and Jesus said, "If I am lifted up from the earth, will draw all men to Myself." (John 12:32) Christian orphan care, foster care, and adoption are included in James 1:27. They not only bring God's love to orphan children; they glorify God and draw others to Jesus Christ.

I know a family who has adopted ten children, and I was dining with them in a restaurant one day when a total stranger stopped by our table and said that he was so blessed and inspired by their example that he wanted to pay for all of their meals. Whether intentional or not, his compliments to the family glorified God. Later, they told me that incidents like this are common for them.

Pastor John Piper says, "Adoption is the most beautiful display of God's grace" and "is the purpose of the universe." [8a] Ephesians 5:27 says that Jesus actually wants to share some of His glory with His bride, the church, because He wants the church to look beautifully attractive to the world, reflecting and radiating the fragrance of His love for all mankind (Matt. 5:16; 2 Cor. 2:15).

Adoption not only blesses orphan children but also touches the hearts of others who are often inspired simply by hearing that someone cares enough to adopt an otherwise unwanted child. I have actually heard people say, "My, what a wonderful thing you're doing. The world needs more people like you." Whether intentionally or not, they have just glorified God because of what they observed, just like the man in the restaurant above with the ten adopted children.

If someone says that to you, be prepared to reply, "What the world really needs is more people like Jesus Christ." You'll be amazed at what may happen next. You can capitalize on an opportunity to pray with them, and people who glorify God in this manner are open to hearing the gospel. Be prepared to introduce them to Jesus Christ and share how they too can become a child of God by adoption! I've seen it happen! It suddenly becomes relevant to share the good news of adoption with them. This is how our Father's business plan is carried out!

Adoption as Ministry

Adoption ministries address many areas of concern for the needs of orphan children and can be as diverse as the churches which operate them. Regardless of their various personalities, there is a great need for the ministries to be organized, have a face that people can see, and have a person to reach out to for answers. In every church I visit, I find families who already want to adopt, but many of them need financial assistance to make adoption affordable. I also encounter people who have thought about adopting but lack the confidence to move forward. If this is your situation, be encouraged and praise the Lord. He has called faithful people everywhere who have the means and the desire to help, and when they learn about the ministry value of adoption, many are delighted to help families in their own church and community. Adoption ministry instills confidence in families that enables them to proceed with adoption and networks them with others who can help provide necessary resources to ensure their success in adopting.

Too often, orphan care and adoption are viewed as social welfare rather than ministry, and many want to invest church resources in something more evangelistic. There is nothing more evangelistic. Jesus Christ came into the world to bring spiritual orphans into God's family by way of adoption. The Bible is filled with instructions and commands for God's people to continually minister to orphans, both physical and spiritual orphans, all for a singular evangelistic purpose, "so that they might receive the adoption as sons" (Gal. 4:5).

Foster Care

Much overlooked is the ministry of foster care, which is another important aspect of orphan ministry. After licensing by a government agency, foster families care for children in need, and the child has a chance to experience the workings of a real family while bypassing orphanage care. Though often mistaken for adoption, foster care ministers to children who have been legally removed from their home or in some other way have lost their home or family and are awaiting court decisions about their permanent placement. Some may eventually be returned to their biological family, or to extended family members, while others await permanent placement by adoption.

Many foster children need and want to be adopted just as much as children in orphanages. A significant percentage of foster families actually end up adopting a foster child, while others find foster care a rewarding ministry to children while they await adoption into someone else's family. Christian foster families are in great demand, and you could make an important contribution to convince a foster child that God really does love them. Even though foster care implies a temporary connection, establishing a lifelong relationship with a foster child might be the best thing you could do to ensure their success in life. Your living example and committed love can also be the best way to help a hurting child comprehend God's love. Both private and government agencies provide training to prepare you for this kind of ministry.

Assisting foster families is another important aspect of orphan ministry. Foster families need encouragement, respect, and support from friends, family, and people like you. Sometimes, they just need someone to watch the children temporarily while they attend to pressing personal business. This is called "respite care." Providing encouragement, transportation, food, clothing, and help with schooling are aspects of this ministry that offer opportunities for participation. A church foster care ministry may be a new idea to you, but it is rightfully the work of the church.

Deciding What to Do

God is the perfect Father who already has a plan in place for each of us. When we prayerfully seek His guidance, He will give it. Isaiah 30:21 says, "Your ears will hear a word behind you saying, 'This is the way, walk in it.'" The fact that we hear the word behind us seems to suggest that we are walking in the wrong direction and need to turn and go the Lord's way! Too often, we pray with wrong motives, asking God to bless our plans instead of asking God what His plans are for our lives. Often, He answers, "Wait" or "No," which we usually misinterpret to mean that He didn't answer our prayer. Sometimes, God's guidance only comes after much prayer and fasting (Ezra 8:23; Dan. 9:3; Acts 13:3). Other times, His answer may be delayed by spiritual warfare (Dan. 10:12–13 delayed twenty-one days). Sometimes, God waits to see if we are qualified in the areas of determination and perseverance. He may even send us on a side trip for an educational experience to give us the missing qualifications needed for the ultimate plan He has in store for our future.

In addition to prayerfully seeking God's guidance, there is wisdom and victory in a multitude of counselors (Prov. 11:14; 15:22; 24:6). Seeking godly advice from fellow Christians is always part of God's way of speaking to us.

Lessons from the Children

A very young girl was abused by her alcoholic father and abandoned along a highway by her mother. Years later, after Torey Hayden had finally proven to this child that she loved her enough to play for keeps, the girl wrote this beautiful and very insightful poem that speaks volumes about how it feels to be an orphan.

All the rest came. They tried to make me laugh. They played their games with me. Some games for fun and some for keeps.

And then they went away, leaving me in the ruins of games, not knowing which were for keeps and which were for fun, and leaving me alone with the echoes of laughter that was not mine.

Then you came with your funny way of being not quite human, and you made me cry, and you didn't seem to care if I did.

You just said the games are over, and waited until all my tears turned into joy.[21]

This poem so accurately describes my own experience working with the children in the orphanage. The fun and games were over when they finally realized that I wasn't playing for keeps.

Adoption is not a game. Adoption is for keeps.

Chapter 5 Reflections

1. Discuss with your group the things churches should do, things you should do.

2. Write a list of your gifts and talents that could be applied to orphan care and adoption.

Ways to Participate in the Family Business of Orphan Care

- Pray for orphans in your land on a regular basis.
- Give clothing and food to orphan ministries.
- Offer personal hands-on assistance to orphanages and social workers.
- Financially support an orphanage.
- Become a foster parent or a foster grandparent.
- Organize and lead church outreach visits to orphanages.
- Work for an agency that cares for orphans.
- Become an active member of a group that supports orphan care.
- Participate in a medical outreach to an orphanage.
- Teach about adoption in churches and Sunday school on radio and TV.
- Conduct adoption forums or organize a multichurch adoption information meeting.
- Adopt a child.
- Give adoption reading material to someone who is considering adoption.
- Help a family you know to raise funds to pay adoption expenses.
- Start an adoption ministry in your church to help many families adopt.

- Professionals can provide adoption related services.
- Contractors can help adoptive families add a necessary extra room.
- Christian missionaries are needed to plant adoption ministries in churches everywhere.
- Read the resource materials found at Home for Good Foundation website entitled
  "Starting and growing your church adoption support ministry" (www.hfgf.org > Ministry Resources > Adoption Ministry Manual > Download pdf).

Chapter 6

Orphan Care and Adoption as Ministry: Some Biblical Bases for Adoption

A Prayer and Scripture to Begin Your Lesson

Thank You, Father, for this opportunity to be a part of Your family business. I pray that You will make it clear to me what role You have for me and empower me to carry out Your desires.

> So we fasted and earnestly prayed that our God would take care of us, and He heard our prayer.
>
> —*Ezra 8:23 NLT*

Lack of understanding of the need for adoption is very common, and you can even find orphanages where the children are not being processed to become eligible for adoption. Until now, you may have never known how desperately orphan children need and want to belong to a loving family. Most people would define orphan ministry as caring for children in an orphanage or foster home, and that was my own definition until after I had worked in an orphanage for a couple of years. Most of us never think about adoption as ministry or as a way of caring for orphans.

Each year, millions of children around the world join the ranks of those who will never be adopted. Many other children in institutions are not legally adoptable, and caring for all of them is very important. However, orphanages and foster homes should be viewed as stepping-stones leading to the ultimate goal of returning a child to his or her birth family, or relatives, if at all possible, or permanent placement in a family via adoption. We must continue to support orphanages and foster care, but we must place a much stronger emphasis on permanent homes for all children.

Some Biblical Bases for Adoption

"Thy will be done, in earth as it is in heaven" (Matt. 6:10 KJV). There are no spiritual orphans in heaven, only spiritually adopted children, and Jesus Himself said, "I will not leave you as orphans" (John 14:18). Adoption is the best way to demonstrate God's love for orphan children, and it accomplishes His will on earth by living example. Helping other families adopt emulates Jesus' heavenly example of paying the cost for our spiritual adoption.

Many of us have been raised to relate to God as a Father to be revered, and even feared, but God wants us to know that He is also the adoring Daddy that many of us never had. I weep in humble joy when I consider that I am a child of God and that He is my adoring Daddy, the perfect Father, who can't wait to forgive this prodigal son. I couldn't make it without knowing this one, simple truth about God. It's one of the most loving images of God I can imagine, but too many orphan children have a distorted image of God. If this applies to you and you've not already done so, now would be a good time to read *The Father's Love Letter* in appendix A.

I discovered, from years of experience in the orphanage, why so many children cannot accept the idea of God as a perfect, loving Daddy. To speak of a loving Father God to an orphan child who has been abused, abandoned, sexually molested, or neglected by his or her own father can easily evoke pain and anger. It's nearly impossible, or difficult at best, for such a child to comprehend the word *love* or to trust anyone as a loving father, unless someone demonstrates to him or her by living example what a loving father really is.

It's hard for an orphan child to comprehend a loving Father God when their image of father evokes pain, anger, or fear. How can they comprehend God's love if they have never experienced a father's love? How can orphan children believe "My God will supply all your needs according to His riches in Glory in Christ Jesus" (Phil. 4:19) while their need for home, family, and belonging remains unfulfilled? How can a boy trust that God will never leave or forsake him, when he has already been abandoned and left to languish in an institution? How can a girl believe that Jesus loves her when she doesn't believe I love her? How can I convince orphan children I love them if I leave them in an orphanage? (1 John 3:17–18).

"If you love me, why don't you adopt me?" My not adopting the children led them to believe that I didn't love them at all. How can we answer the cry of the orphan who asks, "If God loves me, why am I an orphan?" Does this mean that we should stop caring for children in institutions? Of course not! That could only happen in a perfect world. We must find a better way to give every orphan child a sense of belonging that seems to be possible only in a committed, permanent relationship with other human beings.

The Bible challenges the sincerity of our love if we refuse to help fulfill the needs that God brings to our attention. "Whoever has the world's goods, and sees his brother in need and closes his heart against him, how does the love of God abide in him?" (1 John 3:17). The very next verse gives us the answer to this rhetorical question: love must be more than just words; it must be action that demonstrates God's love by living example.

True Religion

In 1 John 3:18 we read, "Little children, let us not love with word or with tongue, but in deed and truth." James 1:27 is an example of living the gospel in deed and in truth that can reach more orphans than preaching the gospel to them. This verse is frequently quoted regarding caring for orphan children, but its deeper meaning is often overlooked. "External religious worship that is pure and unblemished in the sight of God the Father is this: to visit and help and care for the orphans and widows in their affliction and need, and to keep oneself unspotted and uncontaminated from the world" (James 1:27 AB).

James also tells us in chapter 2, verses 15–17, that our faith is useless if we don't do something to fulfill the needs we discover. The following statement, written by Pastor Kefa Sempangi of Uganda, so aptly describes "true religion" that is so relevant to these key verses in James and 1 John 3:17–18.

> Every Sunday for two years, I left early from my dormitory room at the university to collect the children from their impoverished villages and walk them to church. Every Sunday, I taught them in Sunday school of their loving Father in heaven, and of Jesus who had become poor that they might be rich. And every Sunday, I walked them home again, feeling that I had justified myself as a religious teacher. I was not ashamed to say to these children, "Depart in peace, be ye warmed and filled." I was not ashamed to leave them in their destitute condition. To me, they were only souls to save. I had no eyes to see their physical suffering. I met people at my point of expertise, my knowledge of the Scripture, but Jesus met people at their point of need. When a blind man asked Him to restore his eyes, Jesus did not give him religion. He gave him his sight.
>
> This realization brought with it a new understanding of the importance of witchcraft among my people. We were a needy people and could not afford to be answered in abstractions. "Truth" for a non-Westernized African does not refer to a

statement's correspondence with fact. A religion is true if it works, if it meets all the needs of the people. Religion that speaks only to a man's soul and not to his body is not true."[22]

Pastor Sempangi went on to share that his father explained to him why the Christians in his village could not compete with the witch doctor, because they were focused only on evangelism while avoiding activities that are often labeled "social gospel." In other words, the Christians were only ministering to people's souls but not attending to their bodies and their physical and emotional needs.

Here's another Scripture that adds to this discussion." Matthew 7:9–10 says, "Or what man is there among you who, when his son asks for a loaf, will give him a stone? Or if he asks for a fish, he will not give him a snake, will he?" When children are longing for a home and family, should we give them an orphanage?

I'm convinced that the children I worked with in the orphanage didn't believe that I loved them because I didn't adopt them, and my religion wasn't true. If the religion we practice isn't true, how can we expect orphan children to believe our doctrine?

Is it any wonder that many children in orphanages can't relate to what we commonly call "The Gospel?" To them, our religion is not true because our activities are not truly demonstrating the Gospel. The children we worked with wanted to know, "If God loves *me*, why am I an orphan? If *you* love me, why don't you adopt me?" If we don't answer these questions to their satisfaction, how can we expect them to believe our doctrine?

Do you ever wonder why James 1:27 is the only reference to pure and undefiled religion in the entire Bible? Let's take a deeper look into the meaning of this key verse. Does your vision of visiting or caring for orphans ever look or sound anything like the following?

An orphan's foremost affliction, or distress, is not belonging to a family, and the word *visit* means far more than just a social call to an orphanage. *Visit* in the original Greek, *episkeptomai (Strong's Concordance* #1980a), means to go in person to "inspect and select" (for the purpose of discovering someone's needs and to "select" for the purpose of helping to fulfill the needs we discover).

God set the example when He visited us as spiritual orphans. Luke 1:68 says, "Blessed be the Lord God of Israel, for He has visited us and accomplished redemption for His people." Why did He do this? "So that we might receive the adoption as sons" (Gal. 4:5). Luke uses the same Greek word for *visit* that James used in 1:27. God visited us in our affliction so that He might deliver us from it. He inspected us, saw our need for redemption, and selected us for adoption into His family. God wants us to visit orphans in their affliction so we will discover their desperate need for love, home, and family. He showed us by His example that fully delivering orphans from affliction includes adoption.

We can best rescue orphans from their affliction by adopting or by helping other families adopt. In the meantime, we must continue to love and provide for the needs of those who remain as orphans.

After hearing one of our staff teach about the biblical basis for adoption ministry at a pastors conference in Zzana, Uganda, Pastor Daniel Ouma shared his insight about how the following Scriptures could very well be describing the church and her involvement in ministry to orphans and widows. After the conference, many of the sixty-two pastors and church leaders who attended were discussing how this kind of true religion is missing in the Ugandan church

today. Notice the references to widows, orphans, and the poor in the
following verses from Job 29 (NLT).

> In those days my cows produced milk in abundance, and
> my olive groves poured out streams of olive oil. Those
> were the days when I went to the city gate and took my
> place among the honored leaders. The young stepped aside
> when they saw me, and even the aged rose in respect at my
> coming. The princes stood in silence and put their hands
> over their mouths. The highest officials of the city stood
> quietly, holding their tongues in respect. All who heard
> of me praised me. All who saw me spoke well of me. For
> (because) I helped the poor in their need and the orphans
> who had no one to help them. I helped those who had lost
> hope, and they blessed me. And I caused the widows' hearts
> to sing for joy. All I did was just and honest. Righteousness
> covered me like a robe, and I wore justice like a turban ...
> Everyone listened to me and valued my advice. They were
> silent as they waited for me to speak.

We learned from Pastor Daniel that if we view this incredible
picture of Job's influence and position in his community as an
illustration of the church's potential for influence in this world,
we may have discovered something that God is encouraging us
to reconnect with and embrace. Job received this great honor and
respect from his community *because* he helped the poor and the
widows who were crying for help, and he rescued orphans who were
not being helped by anyone (Job 29:12). However, Job did more
than rescue orphans. Verse 31:18 tells us that he adopted orphans and
raised them as a father. God praises Job as a blameless and upright
man and says there is no one like him in all the earth (Job 1:8).
Could the abundance that Job enjoyed in verse 29:6 illustrate the
glory and lasting fruit of the church if she were to fully embrace and
act on James 1:27? Has the church missed for so long the blessings

God intended for her to receive when she gives to orphans the things they really need like home, family, love, and a sense of belonging?

Could these simple acts of love, commitment, and practical support become the "lens" or "storefront" of the church that people would look through, enabling them to see Jesus more clearly? Matthew 5:16 indicates that they will indeed.

What a great witness to be able to share when people praise you for helping widows and orphans or ask why you do these strange things. Here's what I might say:

> When no one cared about me, when friends and relatives deserted me and my father told me I would never amount to anything, I felt like an orphan myself. Then Jesus offered to pay for my adoption into God's family, and when I accepted His offer and became a Child of God, I felt love, forgiveness, and acceptance like never before in my life. Jesus doesn't just talk about loving me; He constantly proves it by His presence and His example. Jesus paid for my adoption and that inspires me to want to bless widows and help pay for someone else's adoption. Now that I've experienced how joyful it is to follow His example, I just want to keep doing more of it. That's why I want to share how you too can become a child of God and how you can find real joy and meaning and peace in your life. This world isn't perfect, but heaven is!

Let's remember the model that Jesus gave us when He willingly shed His blood on the cross to pay for our adoption. Also, recall from chapter 1 that not all are called to adopt, but anyone can love and minister to orphan children by helping other families adopt. This can be especially meaningful when the families we help are in our own home church. Families who choose to adopt encounter many obstacles, and it is clearly a ministry to offer the kind of assistance that will ensure their success. Adoption should not be only for the rich. Consider Galatians 6:2 to bear one another's burdens. Adopting families deserve all the help they can get, especially in developing countries where families need help just to put another plate on their table (Matt. 10:10).

Helping them raise funds for adoption expenses may be a new idea to you, but it's biblical and is an important part of orphan ministry. We have already mentioned that Christian families who adopt should be thought of as missionaries. Adoption ministry answers the question in Romans 10:15 regarding missionaries: "How will they go unless they are sent?"

Without senders, many Christian families will not be able to adopt. Those who help with financial support are just as important as those who adopt. The Bible says in 1 Samuel 30:24–25 that all team members receive equal credit for the victory. Helping other families adopt is far more than just a good thing to do. It can literally be a matter of eternal life or death for many orphans who have never experienced the love of a family. Adoption by a Christian family may be their only chance to learn how much God loves them.

A Cost-Effective Solution for Adoption

Many sermons teach us that Jesus' death on the cross was an incredibly extravagant gift that paid for our salvation and adoption into God's eternal family, and they challenge us to practice the same extravagant love for our neighbor, and extravagant giving to support the work of the church. Yet many still believe that adoption is an extravagant luxury, and they see no reason to help fund someone else's luxury, implying that orphans are not worthy of extravagant love. None of us are worthy of Jesus' extravagant love, but He gave it to us anyway. Extravagance is the only model Jesus gave us for loving others. "Freely you have received, freely give" (Matt. 10:8).

The cost of international adoption can certainly seem extravagant. However, helping foreign nationals adopt children in their own country and culture makes adoption a very cost-effective solution. For example, in the Philippines, we are able to help as many as twenty-five Filipino families adopt a child for the same total cost as raising only one child in an orphanage, (for an average of 10 years). Also, nearly twenty Filipino families can adopt a child for the same total cost as only one international adoption by an American family. In Uganda, there is almost no cost at all for the actual adoption process, and countless Ugandan families are eager to adopt if only they could afford to feed another child in their family. Simply helping these families with a way to feed more children could result in a significant reduction in the orphan population in Uganda.

From a practical standpoint, a successfully adopted child is no longer a burden on society. We can spend money on adoption to empty an existing one-hundred-bed orphanage and immediately house an additional one hundred orphans, without spending a dime to build a new orphanage. Furthermore, adoption can empty the same orphanage over and over again. If we spend money to build a new orphanage, it will soon be full and the number of orphans will continue to increase. If we focused more resources on empowering families who already want to adopt, we could make room to care for thousands, or perhaps even millions, more children in existing orphanages everywhere.

Since 1998, I have been observing an increasing number of governments expressing their strong preference for children to be adopted in their own country and culture. Several countries have already closed their borders to international adoption for any number of reasons, some of them extremely controversial. I personally believe that international adoption will soon become so difficult and costly that it will no longer be a viable option. Corruption, human trafficking, wars, and other political factors could eventually contribute to the total demise of international adoption. I believe we need to prepare for this eventuality by investing as much as possible in establishing adoption as a ministry in evangelical churches in countries around the world. The families who want to adopt are already there!

A Special Word for Pastors

Pastors should not feel any pressure or guilt for not adopting, especially if they are not called by God to adopt. There is also no pressure for anyone to recruit others to adopt. The Holy Spirit is the only qualified recruiter, and He has already called millions of families in churches around the world who are willing and eager to adopt.

In Proverbs 31:8, the church is called to speak up for those who cannot speak for themselves. A pastor's endorsement, or lack thereof, carries considerable influence, either positive or negative. Your endorsement, coupled with teaching that adoption is ministry and evangelism, validated with what God's Word says about orphan care and adoption, can be your gifts and blessings to orphan children. By endorsing a ministry that offers to empower the families in your church who are already called to adopt, you will discover hidden evangelists in your congregation who are eager to bring the gospel to orphan children by living example. Your encouragement will also inspire others to become involved in ministry and evangelism in ways they never thought possible. Every Christian needs to understand that adoption is an integral part of the gospel, and the gospel is incomplete if it fails to include the doctrine of adoption. People need to be taught that adoption can provide the fertile soil in the life of a child where the gospel can take root and thrive. Dr. Russell Moore, former dean of the school of theology at the Southern Baptist Theological Seminary, wrote, "The first step to becoming an adoption friendly church must begin in the pulpit." [23]

When the church recognizes the evangelistic value of adoption and embraces it as ministry equal to any other evangelistic activity, it will begin to make a significant difference in the global orphan crisis. When it fully directs the sacred portion of the tithe, the world will take notice and God will be glorified (Matt. 5:16). Unprecedented church growth would be the natural result.

God has exceedingly blessed the church with this new ministry. In all of church history, there has never been a more willing army of evangelists than can be found in the number of Christian families in churches around the world who already want to adopt. The church needs only to equip and empower them to carry out their calling. In many cases, all a pastor needs to do is to endorse adoption ministry and teach the congregation that it truly is ministry.

Pastor John MacArthur says, "Every pastor should consider the responsibility he has in making adoption a priority for the church as a viable representation of the gospel doctrine of adoption."[24]

Another thing so amazing about adoption ministry is the significant number of people outside the church who are willing to help fund the ministry. They are so impressed with the concept of proactively helping families adopt that they can't refrain from participating, and glorifying God just as Matthew 5:16 says they will. Capitalizing on their godly response can lead to very healthy church growth, and they are open to hearing how they too can become a child of God.

Concerns about the Church Budget

We've heard from many adoption ministry advocates who have encountered concerns from leadership about potential harm to the church budget. I encourage church leaders to study the Scriptures and specifically seek God's direction regarding proactive ministries for widows and orphans. Rediscover God's promise of overflowing blessing for obedience in this area. We've heard many reports of increased giving, designated specifically for ministry to widows and orphans! Some of those reports include very large donations! I believe that in the spirit of the sacred portion offering, church funds could rightfully be used to help church families adopt. Another portion could be directed toward meeting the needs of widows in the church and community. This would be a good time to review the section on the sacred portion in chapter 4.

Conflict of Interest

We have encountered several pastors and their wives who feel called to adopt and who also need financial assistance for adoption. They all seem to share a common fear that asking their congregation for extra financial support to help them pay for adoption expenses is a conflict of interest. I respect the caution and humility this demonstrates, but I strongly believe this gives a pastor an excellent opportunity to be a true role model in regard to adoption ministry, and he can challenge the congregation to follow his example.

According to IRS guidelines, it would only be a conflict of interest if the financial assistance were offered exclusively to the pastor and no one else on the church staff or members of the congregation. It is not the pastor, but rather an orphan child, desperately in need of a family, who is the ultimate beneficiary of any adoption grants or fundraising. This fact alone should remove any shadow of concern about a conflict of interest to help a pastor adopt. If the pastor is the first person in the church who will receive financial support for adoption, he should make it clear that any member of the staff or congregation will be given equal consideration for such support. This is your golden opportunity to endorse adoption ministry to everyone in the church.

Engaging the Congregation

Adoption, orphan care, and foster care should be official ministries of the church. Periodic preaching of the Scriptures found in this Bible study could help these ministries to become a part of the global mission strategy of the church, and the Holy Spirit will call those whom He chooses to be part of them.

Here are some other things a pastor can do that will encourage others to be involved in these ministries:

- Preach the gospel in the context of adoption (Gal. 4:4–5; John 1:12; Eph. 1:4–5).
- Enthusiastically endorse adoption ministry, orphan care, and foster care from the pulpit during regular worship services.
- Teach about the plight of orphan children and their need for love, family, and belonging.
- Inform the congregation of the priority for these ministries and the church's commitment to help families adopt.
- Encourage members to sponsor an orphanage and become personally involved with the children.
- Encourage the entire congregation to help sponsor adoption expenses for families who need assistance.
- Celebrate, and affirm, adoptive families and their children in front of the entire congregation when appropriate.

- Allow use of church facilities for meetings or fundraising activities related to adoption ministry.
- Treat adopting families as missionaries, and identify them to the congregation as such.
- Encourage other related ministries, such as one that could provide post adoption support.
- Network with local businesses that will partner with you to support orphan ministry and adoption.
- Incorporate the adoption resolution found in appendix D, as an official position statement of your church.
- Participate in an annual "Orphan Sunday" event on the first Sunday in November. See www.orphansunday.org. Numerous resources are available on the Orphan Sunday website to enhance your Orphan Sunday event and your church's adoption ministry.

Lessons from the Children

I recall one particular adoption where I had the privilege of transporting the parents to and from the orphanage and helping them with other local transportation while in the Philippines. When they picked up their new little guy, it was a great occasion. He was cheerful, excited, and well prepared by the staff, and he couldn't wait to go. But guess what. There was an older child who lingered around doing what so many do, trying to be the center of attention too, trying to soak up the fun and excitement of the moment. He showed great interest in the younger boy being adopted, making sure that he was safe and comfortable with his new parents, like a true and caring big brother might be. He was front and center during the send-off as well. After the family was settled in their home back in the USA, they called us to ask, "Was that other boy available?" He did his job well, his wooing paid off, he won their hearts, and they were coming back to adopt him. He would truly become the big brother he had only dreamed about.

I also recall how much this family had sacrificed to adopt this child, and how many years they had waited and prayed for him, beginning years before he was even born! This was a defining moment in my life when I heard the Spirit speaking to my heart. "Families like this deserve all the help we can give them!"

There was something else very unique about this adoption experience with this young boy. He seemed to be able to speak, but he rarely ever spoke a word to anyone, and this actually caused another potential adoptive family to reject him. He was quite capable of communicating without words. This could have been his way of hiding his feelings about not belonging to anyone. Perhaps he had no desire to speak to anyone who had no interest in adopting him.

It was so obvious from the moment he first met his new parents that he instinctively knew exactly what he needed and wanted, and they were it! He never did learn his native Filipino language, but within a few weeks of arriving at his new home in the USA, he had learned the language and was speaking as though making up for lost time!

Chapter 6 Reflections

1. Where does the Bible specifically tell us we should adopt orphan children? Do you think James 1:27 and James 2:15–17 are sufficient biblical evidence? Is there even more evidence. Read 2 Timothy 3:16–17 before answering this question.

2. Is adoption the responsibility of believers individually, the church corporately or both?

   "What a pity we plan to do only the things we can do by ourselves!" said A. W. Tozer.

   What happens to us all when we help others and when we allow others to help us?

3. What does our culture tell us about adoption? Can you envision yourself now being able to be a positive force when discussing the doctrine of adoption as a godly model for orphan care when the subject arises?

4. Watch the John Piper five-minute video: http://www. youtube.com/watch?v=CIKehK1lSFY.

Chapter 7

Advice for Families Who Adopt and Those Who Minister to Them

A Prayer for Those Considering Adoption

> God places the lonely in families.
>
> —Ps. 68:6 NLT

Dear Father God, use this study to expand my vision and to overcome my uncertainties. Holy Spirit, give me wisdom far beyond my own understanding and the courage to act upon that wisdom. I thank You for this opportunity.

Adoption of orphan children by a Christian family is a perfect example of a powerful expression of living out the gospel. However, with any true expression of the gospel comes the probability of attack by enemies who do not want God's plans to prevail. When you choose to adopt, you will be better prepared if you are equipped with the whole armor of God. Ephesians 6:10–18 is God's solution for protecting us from the trials and attacks that come. It applies to adoption as much as it applies to anything we do.

Counseling and additional resources are available; however, adoption counseling from a biblical perspective may be difficult to find. Although the situation is improving, many pastors today may not have sufficient practical knowledge or education about orphans and adoption and may not have the personal experience to draw from. You can learn from other adoptive parents, or family members and friends, who believe in what you are doing and will give of their time and energy to encourage you. Proverbs 11:14, 15:22, and 24:6 inform us that there is wisdom and success in a multitude of counselors. The family of God plays a vital role in helping families with their decision to adopt, as well as with logistical help. There are good people out there who are ready and willing to help! You can learn how to be open about adoption, and how to be open with the children you adopt. You can even use conversations about adoption to share the gospel, using adoption as a living example.

Thankfully, there are good Christian materials, and many scholarly writers who have personal experiences they are eager to share, and their numbers are growing. Some are listed in appendix G.

This study may be God's way of preparing you to become a resource person and mentor for others. Once you have the biblical knowledge, you will know how to discern the advice of others. When properly prepared, you can answer objections or negative comments from well-meaning but uninformed friends and even strangers.

Many people don't understand adoption and they may even challenge you with questions that test your motivation and resolve. You may not always have the right answer, but you can become a witness on the spot by saying, "I don't know the exact answer to that question. Forgive me for needing to get back to you on that, but I can tell you right now, if God was willing to sacrifice His very own Son to adopt me, I'm sure there must be something right about what I'm doing."

Looking for ways to answer challenges helps others overcome their lack of understanding about adoption, and brings more people closer to the heart of God. Knowing that Jesus was adopted is evidence that God does not consider adopted people to be "second class." Anyone who is struggling with adoption and their identity should take great comfort in this truth.

Concerns and comments will come in many forms. Some will worry about family inheritance and what must be shared with other children already in the family. Others may worry if they will like this new child in their home and wonder if they can truly love them the same as they would love their biological children. Still others may wonder if they can parent a child with an unknown background. "God has not given us a spirit of fear, but of power and of love and of a sound mind" (2 Tim. 1:7 KJV). Questions and challenges can be healthy, but we must ask ourselves if they come from common sense, negative attitudes, or fear.

When people challenge you or ask difficult questions about adoption, respect the one who asks, because he or she has been kind enough to reveal what's on their mind, rather than just thinking bad thoughts. You can honestly say, "I'm glad you asked that question." Now you have an open door to tell them about adoption, God's heart for orphans, and the power of the blood of Jesus Christ to cleanse us from all sin. This may even be the right time to share how they too can become a child of God by way of adoption.

I've learned that the objections and challenges I encounter, regarding adoption, can easily be answered by looking to God's Word. Even those who are not open to God's leading will be impacted by a biblical truth. The Bible tells us that God's Word will not return to Him void or empty, without accomplishing His purposes (Isa. 55:11).

Ephesians 1:3–5 clearly teaches that we have been adopted into God's family solely through His gracious act of love and have been given access to all of the blessings, privileges and rewards of His love. In response should we not act accordingly by exalting Christ through various models of care that demonstrate love and concern and, when appropriate, the adoption of orphans. These acts are not based on results, pragmatic methodology, or psychological principles, but are based on the nature of God's love for us and the response due Him. Is this not the best model that we should be pursuing? We should strive to provide the best care, love, instruction and opportunities for orphans, just as God has done for us." [25]

Common Misconceptions about Adoption

Adoption is social welfare rather than ministry. Some even believe that adoption does not belong in the church! Our church mandate is clear; it is to win souls. You have already read that adoption is an integral part of the gospel and how children can comprehend the gospel in the context of their own physical adoption. When the church recognizes and capitalizes on the ministry and evangelistic nature of adoption, she will begin to make a significant difference in the world's orphan crisis and will make great strides toward fulfilling the great commission and filling more churches. The gospel is simply incomplete if it fails to include adoption.

Adoption is an extravagant luxury. Jesus' death on the cross to pay for our adoption into God's family was the most extravagant gift ever given. We should be willing to offer extravagant love to helpless orphans and widows when it is within our means to do so, because God wants us to emulate His extravagant love. "Freely you received; freely give" (Matt. 10:8). Adoption should be a part of the global mission strategy of every evangelical church. Adoption provides the fertile soil for an orphan child where the gospel can take root and thrive. Giving an orphan child the gift of love, a home, a family, and a sense of belonging gives him or her an excellent opportunity to become a child of God. Yes, the family will surely be blessed in the process, but it's the child who is the ultimate beneficiary of any assistance or financial support given to help a family adopt. Adoption is not luxury, it is spiritual warfare against the forces of evil who seek to destroy children and families.

Adoption is unnecessary. It's cheaper to raise children in an orphanage. You have already heard the argument against this and can now readily provide an answer to this misconception. Consider the much lower cost of helping foreign nationals adopt children in their own country and culture. Recall our experience of being able to help Filipino families adopt twenty to twenty-five Filipino children for the same cost as raising only one child in an orphanage. Remember, once adopted, a child is no longer a charity case. That charitable concern and possible lifelong burden on society has been eliminated.

It's better to get orphan children saved than to get them adopted. Statistics show that the vast majority of orphan children who are never adopted never get saved. The reality is that a much higher percentage of children "get saved" as a result of being adopted by a loving Christian family who will show them the gospel and God's love by living example. Orphan children can relate to becoming a child of God in the context of their own physical adoption. Adoption really is an excellent way to get orphan children saved. Galatians 4:4–5 tells us that adoption is the way that everyone gets saved.

Children are orphans because they have bad blood. The significance of blood is very real and this challenge presents a great opportunity to share with people what God's Word says about bad blood. The Bible tells us in Romans 3:23 (NLT) that "all have sinned and fall short of God's glorious standard" (of perfection). We are all born with a sinful nature. Sin is "in our blood," so to speak. In other words, our blood is no different from the blood of orphan children. We all have bad blood, and that's why "all our righteous deeds are like a filthy garment" (Isa. 64:6).

Praise God that "the blood of Jesus Christ His Son cleanses us from all sin" (1 John 1:7). Therefore, "what God has cleansed, no longer consider unholy" (Acts 10:15; 11:9). It is not biblical to consider orphans or adoption as unholy, or to stigmatize anyone for having bad blood, for in so doing, we render useless the blood of Jesus Christ. Remember Jesus died to cleanse us from sin, "while we were yet sinners" filled with bad blood (Rom. 5:8). Jesus was willing to give us His name, even though we continue to bring Him shame. How can we, who claim the name of Jesus, be ashamed to give our name to a child whose blood has been cleansed by the blood of Jesus Christ?

One of the greatest displays of God's love is expressed in adoption. God loves us so much that He wants to have a permanent relationship with us, and He formalizes that relationship by adopting us as His special children. He further proves how special adopted children are by making them joint heirs of His kingdom with His only begotten Son, Jesus Christ. Moses, Queen Esther, and Jesus were all adopted as children, and God used them as shining examples of how He feels about children whom He has adopted, to show us how special they are in His kingdom.

Adoption competes for funds that are urgently needed to care for more orphans. We have discovered there are many people who are willing and eager to help others adopt but have no interest in sponsoring orphan care. Many times, it is a one-time contribution rather than ongoing support. There is no competition for these particular funds. Read the next paragraph to learn how adoption actually multiplies the number of children that can be cared for in any existing orphanage at no additional cost.

Adoption by families who already have children takes away a child that could have been adopted by a family who cannot bear biological children. This misconception assumes the demand for adoption exceeds the supply of adoptable children.

The truth is there are over 160 million orphans in the world, but fewer than 20,000 are adopted annually. The supply far exceeds the current demand, and there are thousands of children available for every family that wants to adopt.

Children become angry when they find out they were adopted. That usually only happens if their parents never told them they were adopted. It's generally not a problem when children are told the truth from day one, and their parents are able and willing to answer all their questions. Children are far more likely to be angry that they were abandoned, rather than because they were adopted. Others may be angry at God for allowing whatever terrible thing happened to them, but we all bear scars, they are not unique to orphans or children who have been adopted. Teaching children that Moses, Queen Esther and Jesus were adopted can help them better understand and appreciate their own adoption. It would also be meaningful for them to know that the greatest celebration in the world will happen when God reveals all the children He has adopted, and shows the entire universe how proud He is that we are His children.

Adoption currently represents less than 1 percent of Christian orphan ministry; therefore, we need to invest in building more orphanages. Consider this opposite logic. If we spend the money on adoption instead, then we can empty an existing one-hundred-bed orphanage and immediately house an additional one hundred orphans without spending a dime to build a new orphanage. Furthermore, adoption can empty the same orphanage over and over again. However, if we spend the money to build a new orphanage, it will soon be full, and the number of orphans will continue to increase. If adoption ministry accounted for more than 50 percent of ministry to orphan children, it could make room to care for thousands or perhaps even millions more children in existing orphanages everywhere.

The statements above are in no way intended to degrade or discredit orphan care or those who provide or support it. Our only purpose is to encourage more participation in adoption and to help increase its overall contribution to orphan ministry. We will never begin to solve the world's orphan crisis until adoption becomes a far greater part of the overall orphan ministry matrix than its current insignificant fraction.

I pray that this book has answered all your questions about adoption or will lead you to the God of heaven who can answer them all. Jesus said in John 8:32, "You will know the truth, and the truth will make you free." Anything not of truth is not of God! The truth of God's Word, and truth in our daily lives, indeed brings freedom. It is always better for children and others involved to know the truth about adoption from the very beginning. At times, there may be a need not to talk about it in public, which will vary depending on the needs of the child and the people around you. Many children who were adopted will not have the confidence to stand out in a crowd and will not want to be thought of as different, while other children may be excited to let people know they were adopted. God is proud that we are His children, and we should be as proud about adoption as God is. We should also inspire the same pride in the children we adopt. There are other resources that address these issues in greater depth.

Lessons from the Children

After several years in the orphanage, my wife and I had gained considerable confidence in the adoption process, and the hearts of so many families that were willing to accept a child into their home unconditionally. However, we discovered that the orphanage staff were neglecting some of the children by limiting their time and energy to prepare the adoption paperwork only for the children they assumed that people would want to adopt. They were processing the babies while neglecting the older children.

I began insisting that all children should have their dossiers processed and up-to-date and submitted into the adoption system as quickly as possible. We would provide whatever backup support it took. It was a process of getting old habits and ideas changed and trusting and believing there were families who would adopt the difficult ones. I remember my wife's statement well as she instructed the social worker, "You do your part, and God will take care of the rest."

There were two children with special needs who had been stuck in the orphanage for years. They had no hope, no paperwork, and no future. Those in charge had decided that no one would want them, so why bother to expend the extra work, time, and resources? Processing these older children took staff away from other important duties, but it worked, and those children were adopted very quickly. Every time I read or hear that description—you know, "the unadoptable"—I think of those two children. We did our part, and God took care of the rest.

Chapter 7 Reflections

1. It would be a good idea at this point in the study to spend some time talking about misconceptions and praying about a movement of the Holy Spirit to change hearts and minds.

2. Take time to review some of your comments from previous chapters and discuss what was the most revealing about adoption in general, and the orphan situation as we know it today.

3. Write down a few of the Scriptures that spoke to you the most.

4. Is there any adult, child, or relative you can pray about right now?

5. Is there any action that is burning in your heart that you want to talk about or that you feel called to undertake?

Conclusion

My learning experience about orphans began the first time I asked myself, "What's wrong with this picture?" Then I began asking, "What's wrong with these children? They're acting like they don't appreciate all this good care we're giving them in this orphanage." It wasn't until I learned what Kay Warren said about it that I finally knew the question I should be asking: "What's wrong with *me* that I'm not getting it?" Children just don't want to *be* orphans!

The most frequent reports we hear from people who have visited orphanages describe the words, or the deathly silence,[26] and body language of the children communicating their desperate hunger and need to belong to a loving family. I have experienced this myself numerous times in several orphanages.

Jesus said, "If you love Me, you will keep My commandments" (John 14:15). Also, James 1:27 commands us to care for widows and orphans. James 2:15–17 tells us that faith without works is useless. First John 3:18 confirms my own experience, that love is best demonstrated in action, and if it is not voluntary, it is not perceived as love. Jesus clearly showed us the voluntary nature of love when He said in John 10:18, regarding His own life, "No one has taken it away from Me, but I lay it down on My own initiative." Love goes beyond the call of duty and acts when there is no command. True love is giving that which is not owed. Love is its own mandate (Matt. 22:37–40).

There are clear examples, but no explicit commands, in the Bible to adopt. Love fulfills every command, and adoption is a purely voluntary expression of love (Matt. 22:40). It doesn't matter to the children how we interpret Scriptures. What matters is the way that we respond to the orphan's cry. Our response reveals the condition of our heart. Responding with adoption reflects the heart of God, and orphan children instinctively know that adoption is a true expression of love.

How can we explain the outcomes of institutional care when so many loving people have given so generously to provide for children in institutions? I am convinced that the answer lies not in the quality of the care we give the children but is deeply rooted in how they perceive our care. The secret to this apparent mystery lies in the voluntary nature of love and the need for belonging that God has placed deep in the heart of every human being. Our visits to an orphanage, our attention, our affection, and the food and clothing we provide are all important, necessary, and honoring to God. However, the children are still orphans; their basic need for belonging remains unfulfilled and they desperately want to know "If you love me, why don't you adopt me?" Adoption is a voluntary act. It proves our love, gives a child a sense of belonging, and demonstrates God's love by living example.

The ultimate goal of any orphan ministry should be, whenever possible, to bring the children into God's family. For most orphan children, giving them our heart, our home, our name, and our inheritance is what it will take to make this happen. Therefore, becoming parents to an orphan child can certainly be implied from Paul's comments in 1 Corinthians 9:22. "I have become all things to all men, so that I may by all means save some."

Adoption is a new season in church history, a new paradigm of orphan ministry, and a global movement of the Holy Spirit. It's a ministry that we must not overlook.

Many Christian families long to adopt but are prevented by the cost. Adoption is both ministry and evangelism, because Christian families who adopt are missionaries who bring the gospel and God's love to orphan children by living example. Adoption ministry empowers them to accomplish their mission. Providing financial support for adopting families is the same as sponsoring any other missionaries. When we donate funds to help other families adopt, we are emulating Jesus' sacrifice on the cross to pay for our own adoption.

Spiritual adoption speaks of a personal relationship with a perfect Father who loves us so much that He wants to make us His children and give us an inheritance equal to that of His Son Jesus Christ. What a wonderfully personal way to envision eternal life as God's special little boy or girl. What a simple concept to understand. I stand in fearful awe, and I revere, honor, and serve God. Yet I weep in humble joy when I consider that I am His child and that He is an adoring Father who longs to forgive this prodigal son and restore me to His perfect fellowship so I can relate to Him as my Abba Daddy. I couldn't make it without knowing this one, simple truth about God. It's the most personal expression of His love that I can imagine.

In Ephesians 1:5 we learn that even before God created the world, adoption was His plan to bring us into His family. Adoption is not God's second best, and He was willing to pay an enormous price to prove it. Oh, His extravagant love that He gave us His only Son, Jesus Christ, who willingly shed His blood on the cross to redeem us, so "that we might receive the adoption as sons."

Endnotes

1. Vicar Mark Stibbe. *From Orphans to Heirs.* © *1999* Bible Reading Fellowship (UK) p. 13.

2. R. Albert Mohler, Jr. An endorsement in *Adopted for Life.* Russell D. Moore, © *2009* Crossway Books.

3. Steven Curtis Chapman. "The Great Need." Shaohannah's Hope Foundation, http://www.howtoadopt.org/TheGreatNeed/. Accessed in 2005, paragraph 5

4. Nell Bernstein. "A Sentence of Their Own." Media fellow with the Center on Crime, Communities, and Culture of the Open Society Institute. A weblog: http://www.asentenceoftheirown.com/Essays%20-%20Welfare%20Ref. html Paragraph 5
   See also the following:
   • Madeline Freundlich, Leslee Morris, Emily Blair. "A Return to Orphanages?"
     Center for Adoption Research, University of Massachusetts, July 2004, p. 6, and p. 32.

5. Vicar Mark Stibbe. *From Orphans to Heirs.* © *1999* Bible Reading Fellowship (UK) p. 28.

6. www.somaly.org/ and www.makewaypartners.org/effects.html (no longer accessible on line)

7. Vicar Mark Stibbe. *From Orphans to Heirs.* © *1999* Bible Reading Fellowship (UK) p. 13.

8. Pastor John Piper. Video and Weblog: Bethlehem Baptist Church. Both accessed in 2005–2007.
   a. http://www.youtube.com/watch?v=CIKehK1lSFY
   b. http://www.desiringgod.org/conference-messages/adoption-the-heart-of-the-gospel

9. J.I. Packer. *Knowing God.* © 1993 Hodder and Stoughton. p. 232.

10. Dr. Russell D. Moore. *Adopted for Life.* © *2009* Crossway Books. P. 19.

11. Ken Fong. *Secure in God's Embrace.* © *2003* Intervarsity Press. p. 16.

12. Dr. Russell D. Moore. "Abba Changes Everything." © July 2010 *Christianity Today.* p. 20.
    Also at: http://www.ctlibrary.com/ct/2010/july/10.18.html

13. Francis Lyall. "Legal Metaphors in the Epistles." *Slaves, Citizens, Sons.* © *1984* Zondervan Publishing House. p. 86–88.

14. Ibid. p. 70–71.

15. Ibid. p. 88, paragraph 2.

16. Ibid. p. 83 and 85.

17. Ibid. p. 76.

18. Beth Moore. *Jesus the One and Only.* © *2000* LifeWay Press. p. 15.

19. C. Thomas Davis. *Fields of the Fatherless.* © *2002* Global Publishing Services. p. 52.

20. Madeline Freundlich, Leslee Morris, Emily Blair. "A Return to Orphanages?" Center for Adoption Research, University of Massachusetts, July 2004, p. 6, and p. 32.
    See also the following:
    - Nell Bernstein. "A Sentence of Their Own." Media fellow with the Center on Crime, Communities, and Culture of the Open Society Institute. A weblog: http://www.asentenceoftheirown. com/Essays%20-%20Welfare%20Ref.html Paragraph 5
    - Vicar Mark Stibbe. *From Orphans to Heirs.* © *1999* Bible Reading Fellowship (UK) p. 28.

21. Torey L. Hayden. "Epilogue" *One Child.* © 1980 G. Putnam's Sons. p. 220.

22. F. Kefa Sempangi. *A Distant Grief.* © 1979 G/L Publications, Regal Books Division. p. 22, 90, 91.

23. Dr. Russell D. Moore. *Adopted for Life.* © *2009* Crossway Books. p. 169–177.

24. John MacArthur. An endorsement in *Adopted for Life.* Dr. Russell D. Moore. © 2009 Crossway Books.

25. Daren Beck "The Care of Orphans. Guiding Principles and Best Practices." A position paper for Action International Ministries. http://www.epm.org/ resources/2005/Dec/19/care-orphans-guiding-principles-and-best-practices/.

26. Dr. Russell D. Moore. "Abba Changes Everything." © July 2010 *Christianity Today.* p. 20.
    Also at: http://www.ctlibrary.com/ct/2010/july/10.18.html

Appendix A

The Father's Love Letter

A DVD Available in Over One Hundred Languages

We highly recommend this inspirational video that simulates a love letter from God, written to every person on earth. It is simply a collection of Scriptures which have been paraphrased into everyday language and read aloud as if God Himself is speaking to us. He is! It is a very powerful message that is sure to bring tears to your eyes and love to your heart. It ends with a challenging question that reflects the purpose of this Bible study. "Will *you* be my child?

Following is the full transcript of *The Father's Love Letter* DVD (http://www.fathersloveletter.com/), shared with permission of its author, Barry Adams.

My Child ...

You may not know me, but I know everything about you.
—Psalm 139:1

I know when you sit down and when you rise up.
—Psalm 139:2

I am familiar with all your ways.
—Psalm 139:3

Even the very hairs on your head are numbered.
—Matthew 10:29–31

For you were made in my image.
—Genesis 1:27

95

In me you live and move and have your being.
—**Acts 17:28**

For you are my offspring.
—**Acts 17:28**

I knew you even before you were conceived.
—**Jeremiah 1:4–5**

I chose you when I planned creation.
—**Ephesians 1:11–12**

You were not a mistake, for all your days are written in my book.
—**Psalm 139:15–16**

I determined the exact time of your birth and where you would live.
—**Acts 17:26**

You are fearfully and wonderfully made.
—**Psalm 139:14**

I knit you together in your mother's womb.
—**Psalm 139:13**

And brought you forth on the day you were born.
—**Psalm 71:6**

I have been misrepresented by those who don't know me.
—**John 8:41–44**

I am not distant and angry, but am the complete expression of love.
—**1 John 4:16**

And it is my desire to lavish my love on you.
—**1 John 3:1**

Simply because you are my child and I am your Father.
—1 John 3:1

I offer you more than your earthly father ever could.
—Matthew 7:11

For I am the perfect Father.
—Matthew 5:48; Luke 15:20–24

Every good gift that you receive comes from my hand.
—James 1:17

For I am your provider and I meet all your needs.
—Matthew 6:31–33

My plan for your future has always been filled with hope.
—Jeremiah 29:11

Because I love you with an everlasting love.
—Jeremiah 31:3

My thoughts toward you are countless as the sand on the seashore.
—Psalm 139:17–18

And I rejoice over you with singing.
—Zephaniah 3:17

I will never stop doing good to you.
—Jeremiah 32:40

For you are my treasured possession.
—Exodus 19:5

I desire to establish you with all my heart and all my soul.
—Jeremiah 32:41

And I want to show you great and marvelous things.
—Jeremiah 33:3

If you seek me with all your heart, you will find me.
—Deuteronomy 4:29

Delight in me and I will give you the desires of your heart.
—Psalm 37:4

For it is I who gave you those desires.
—Philippians 2:13

I am able to do more for you than you could possibly imagine.
—Ephesians 3:20

For I am your greatest encourager.
—2 Thessalonians 2:16–17

I am also the Father who comforts you in all your troubles.
—2 Corinthians 1:3–4

When you are brokenhearted, I am close to you.
—Psalm 34:18

As a shepherd carries a lamb, I have carried you close to my heart.
—Isaiah 40:11

One day I will wipe away every tear from your eyes.
—Revelation 21:3–4

And I'll take away all the pain you have suffered on this earth.
—Revelation 21:3–4

I am your Father, and I love you even as I love my son, Jesus.
—John 17:23

For in Jesus, my love for you is revealed.
—John 17:26

He is the exact representation of my being.
—Hebrews 1:3

He came to demonstrate that I am for you, not against you.
—Romans 8:31

And to tell you that I am not counting your sins.
—2 Corinthians 5:18–19

Jesus died so that you and I could be reconciled.
—2 Corinthians 5:18–19

His death was the ultimate expression of my love for you.
—1 John 4:10

I gave up everything I loved that I might gain your love.
—Romans 8:31–32

If you receive the gift of my son Jesus, you receive me.
—1 John 2:23

And nothing will ever separate you from my love again.
—Romans 8:38–39

Come home and I'll throw the biggest party heaven has ever seen.
—Luke 15:7; Luke 15:22–24

I have always been Father, and will always be Father.
—Ephesians 3:14–15 Isaiah 9:6

My question is … Will you be my child?
—John 1:12–13

I am waiting for you.
—Luke 15:11–32 (the parable of the Perfect Father)

Love,

Your Dad (Abba),
Almighty God

Appendix B

How to Become a Child of God, by Adoption

God has already sent His Son, Jesus Christ, to make all the arrangements and to pay for your adoption.

"But when the fullness of the time came, God sent forth His Son, born of a woman, born under the law, so that He might redeem those who were under the law, that we might receive the adoption as sons."
Gal. 4:4–5

"But as many as received Him, to them He gave the right to become children of God."
John 1:12

"But God showed his great love for us by sending Christ to die for us while we were still sinners."
Rom 5:8 (NLT)

"For God so loved the world, that He gave His only begotten Son, that whoever believes in Him shall not perish, but have eternal life."
John 3:16

"God saved you by His special favor when you believed. And you can't take credit for this; it is a gift from God.
Ephesians 2:8–9 (NLT)

In Hebrews 13:5 God says He will never leave or forsake us. You don't need to live like an orphan for one more day. Jesus said, "I will not leave you as orphans, I will come to you." (John 14:18) God chose you to be His child even before you were born. (Eph. 1:4–5) Nothing you could ever do would cause Him to stop loving you. (Rom. 8:38–39) God is waiting for you.

Romans 3:23 says "All have sinned and fall short of the glory of God." Romans 6:23 tells us, "The wages (or penalty) of sin is death, but the free gift of God is eternal life." The only way to receive the free gift of God is to become one of His children. We become a child of God when we accept the fact that Jesus' death on the cross paid the penalty for our sin. Therefore, our spiritual death (separation from God) is no longer necessary when we receive Jesus Christ and become a child of God by way of adoption.

Receiving Jesus Christ means to renounce (turn away from) sin (that means to repent) and, just like the prodigal son did, confess that you are not worthy to be a son anymore because you know you are a sinner. Ask God to forgive your sins, and then read the story of the prodigal son in Luke 15:11–32. Notice how the father in this story could not wait to forgive his son.

These verses tell the story of how God, the perfect Father, wants to forgive us. Receiving Jesus Christ is more than just an intellectual or emotional experience. It is an act of your will in simple child-like faith. Roman 10:9 says, "If you confess with your mouth that Jesus is (your) Lord, and believe in your heart that God raised Him from the dead, you will be saved." To be saved means the same thing as becoming a child of God (Rom. 8:23). It means to be saved from your sins, saved from judgment, and saved from hell.

Once you receive Jesus Christ, then you really are worthy to be God's beloved child. You are worthy because Jesus cleansed you with

His blood, which paid the penalty for all of your sins. Therefore, "What God has cleansed, no longer consider unholy." (Acts 10:15; Acts 11:9)

Appendix C

Appendix C is a collection of excerpts from an unpublished document written by a personal friend, Timothy Sliedrecht, in January 2005, as a first draft of the introduction to his Master's Thesis. It is included herein with his permission. Section 2, Further Excerpts, is from his final version, also with his permission and unpublished as of this writing.

The Need for an Adoption Bible Study

The doctrine of divine adoption is an essential doctrine in the Bible, emphasized in the New Testament and based in the Old Testament. However, as recognized by Angus Stewart,* it is a doctrine that has been neglected in the church and Christian writings, past and present. What's more, it is a doctrine that has seldom been practically applied and manifested in the church. The fact is that physical adoption is a ministry that brings the gospel of adoption to life, emulating God's love in divine adoption, following Christ's command and example to love self-sacrificially, and fulfilling the Great Commission to make disciples of all nations.

Scripture repeatedly reveals God's high value of children, particularly orphaned and oppressed children. In an age where orphans exist in the multitudes and abortion is a universally acceptable practice, physical adoption is a necessary calling and ministry that every Christian must support and every church must promote and embrace. Unfortunately, primarily due to lack of information and resources, most churches have fallen short and only a handful actually have an adoption ministry. This is primarily due to the fact that most of what is written regarding physical adoption involves personal how-to manuals and personal stories. Not much, if anything, even among already established adoption and orphan ministries, has been written on the theology behind, ministry of, and strategy to implement a ministry of physical adoption.

In order to embrace, rather than traditionally neglect, the ministry of physical adoption, Christians and churches need to better appreciate their own divine adoption by God, the biblical view of physical adoption in light of its view of children, orphans, and oppressed, and the necessity of physical adoption today. Also, they need to grasp how physical adoption fulfills the Great Commandment of love and the Great Commission of making disciples of all nations. Lastly, they need to comprehend the ministerial extent of physical adoption and how the church can actually implement and develop an adoption ministry. Only then will Christians and churches embrace adoption as a ministry.

Further Excerpts

Also, considering the fact that the blessings incurred by Christ's death and resurrection go beyond "just" redemption and salvation, using the word *adoption* as opposed to *salvation* or *redemption* in conjunction with God's plan and gospel seems much more true to their meaning, as adoption includes the from and the to. In their verb form, *redemption* and *salvation* are prepositional transitive verbs; more specifically, verbs followed by the preposition *from*. A person can be saved or redeemed *from* something or someone but cannot be saved or redeemed *to* something or someone. Thus, "saving/redeeming from" is only the incomplete first half of God's plan and the gospel. Alternatively, the word *adoption* really includes salvation in that a person can be adopted *from* something or someone yet goes further in meaning in that a person can be adopted *to* sonship and *into* a family. Ultimately, God's plan is for man to *be adopted to sonship and into His family.*

* Angus Stewart, "Adoption: A Theological Exposition of a Neglected Doctrine," *British Reformed Journal*, issue no. 25 (January–March 1999). http://www.britishreformed.org/.

Timothy Sliedrecht and his wife, Angie, are parents of six children: four through adoption and two through biology! They currently serve as missionaries in Soroti, Uganda, with International Teams, promoting and advocating for orphan care and adoption as they share the gospel and God's love with the people of Uganda. You may contact Tim at tim.sliedrecht@iteams.org. His blog is http://sliedrechts.wordpress.com.

Appendix D

On Adoption and Orphan Care:
A Resolution Adopted by the Messengers of
The Southern Baptist Convention
June 23–24, 2009, Louisville, Kentucky

WHEREAS, In the gospel we have received the "Spirit of adoption" whereby we are no longer spiritual orphans but are now beloved children of God and joint heirs with Christ (John 14:18; Romans 8:12–25; Galatians 3:27–4:9; Ephesians 1:5); and

WHEREAS, The God we now know as our Father reveals Himself as a "Father of the fatherless" (Psalm 68:5) who grants mercy to orphans (Deuteronomy 10:18; Hosea 14:3); and

WHEREAS, Our Lord Jesus welcomes the little ones (Luke 18:15–17), pleads for the lives of the innocent (Psalm 72:12–14), and shows us that we will be held accountable for our response to "the least of these brothers of mine" (Matthew 25:40); and

WHEREAS, The Scripture defines "pure and undefiled religion" as "to look after orphans and widows in their distress" (James 1:27); and

WHEREAS, The satanic powers and the ravages of sin have warred against infants and children from Pharaoh to Molech to Herod and, now, through the horrors of a divorce culture, an abortion industry, and the global plagues of disease, starvation, and warfare; and

WHEREAS, Southern Baptists have articulated an unequivocal commitment to the sanctity of all human life, born and unborn; and

WHEREAS, Churches defined by the Great Commission must be concerned for the evangelism of children—including those who have no parents; and

WHEREAS, Upward of 150 million orphans now languish without families in orphanages, group homes, and placement systems in North America and around the world; and

WHEREAS, Our Father loves all of these children, and a great multitude of them will never otherwise hear the gospel of Jesus Christ; now, therefore, be it

RESOLVED, That the messengers to the Southern Baptist Convention meeting in Louisville, Kentucky, June 23–24, 2009, express our commitment to join our Father in seeking mercy for orphans; and be it further

RESOLVED, That we call on each Southern Baptist family to pray for guidance as to whether God is calling them to adopt or foster a child or children; and be it further

RESOLVED, That we encourage our pastors and church leaders to preach and teach on God's concern for orphans; and be it further

RESOLVED, That we commend churches and ministries that are equipping families to provide financial and other resources to those called to adopt, through grants, matching funds, or loans; and be it further

RESOLVED, That we encourage local churches to champion the evangelism of and ministry to orphans around the world, and to seek out ways to energize Southern Baptists behind this mission; and be it further

RESOLVED, That we encourage Southern Baptist churches to join with other evangelical Christians in setting aside a special Sunday each year to focus upon our adoption in Christ and our common burden for the orphans of the world; and be it further

RESOLVED, That we pray what God is doing in creating an adoption culture in so many churches and families can point us to a gospel oneness that is determined not by "the flesh," or race, or economics, or cultural sameness, but by the Spirit, unity, and peace in Christ Jesus; and be it finally

RESOLVED, That we pray for an outpouring of God's Spirit on Southern Baptist congregations so that our churches will proclaim and picture, in word and in deed, that "Jesus loves the little children, all the children of the world."

Authored by Dr. Russell D. Moore
Louisville, Kentucky
http://www.sbc.net/resolutions/amResolution.asp?ID=1194
Copyright © 2009 Southern Baptist Convention. Used by permission.

Bishop Efraim Tendero Endorses the SBC Resolution

Warm greetings in the mighty name of our Lord Jesus Christ!

On behalf of the Philippine Council of Evangelical Churches (PCEC), I am highly endorsing the Southern Baptist Convention Resolution on Adoption and Orphan Care.

PCEC is one with the Southern Baptist Church in deeply valuing the spiritual worth of adoption, and the sanctity of human life.

As Christians, it is our responsibility to care for our orphaned brothers and sisters. We ourselves are "adopted children," spiritually invited by God to share His riches in heaven and being loved by Him as if we were His own. God has shown His supreme love for all kinds of children, including orphans, in Luke 18, and He has commanded us to look after them and answer to their need. Also, by disregarding cultural or racial barriers through adoption, we magnify our being one as a spiritual family with God as our Father.

In a PCEC statement released last July 2008, we had clearly affirmed our belief that life begins at conception and any unborn baby at whatever stage of pregnancy should be cared for and protected. God commanded us to be good stewards of His creation and not just to multiply. Responsible parenthood and care for orphaned children is part of this command. In a world where human life is disrespected through abortion, diseases, and abuse, we commend the foster parents and organizations like the Home for Good Foundation who advocate for orphan children yearning for a loving family, and actively promote their adoption. In their own small ways, they have been good stewards, responding to the cry of millions of orphans suffering worldwide.

I encourage the whole evangelical body to also preach and tell about God's love for the orphans. To the church members, I advise you to discern prayerfully whether you are called to adopt a child or children. This will not only lessen the cries of the yearning but also emphasize our identity as children of God.

God bless you!
Your co-laborer in Christ,

Bishop Efraim M. Tendero
National director, Philippine Council of Evangelical Churches

Appendix E

**The Following List of Thoughts and Actions Was
Published by Saddleback Church in 2012**

163 Million Orphans in the World?

We need to think and act differently. Below are
some ways that those of us at Saddleback Church
are thinking and acting differently.

What we used to think and do for orphans	What we think and do *now*
Pray, pay, and stay away	Go and serve the local church
Go do projects *for* the local church globally	Indigenous church owns, initiates
We're the hero	The local church is the hero
Build orphanages	Empty orphanages
Help	Help without hurting
Give them "things"	Give them ourselves
Place children in orphanages	Unite children to a lifelong family
Measure success by dollars given	Measure success by children in permanent families
Medicate and educate	Cure
Hire a temporary family	Equip a lifelong family
Help orphans find shelter	Help orphans find a mom and dad
Think there weren't enough families	Realize there are more than enough families. 163 million orphans: 2.4 billion Christians = Enough

Work on the orphan crisis	End the orphan crisis through the church and family
Help orphans live a better life as an orphan	Help orphans become sons and daughters
Churches provide leads to donors	Churches provide leads to adoptive families and provide lay social workers, training. and support necessary for success
Churches can't do much to help with adoption globally	Churches can empower other churches to change the world

Let's get to zero orphans!

Used with permission.

Appendix F

Scriptures Related to Adoption, Orphans, Children of God

Orphan (twenty-six instances)

shall not afflict any widow or **orphan**	Exod. 22:22
executes justice for the **orphan** and the	Deut. 10:18
the **orphan** and the widow who are in	Deut. 14:29
and the stranger and the **orphan** and the	Deut. 16:11
the stranger and the **orphan** and the widow	Deut. 16:14
the justice due an alien *or* an **orphan**,	Deut. 24:17
alien, for the **orphan**, and for the widow	Deut. 24:19
alien, for the **orphan**, and for the widow	Deut. 24:20
alien, for the **orphan**, and for the widow	Deut. 24:21
to the **orphan** and to the widow	Deut. 26:12
the alien, the **orphan** and the widow	Deut. 26:13
justice due an alien, **orphan**, and widow	Deut. 27:19
snatch the **orphan** from the breast	Job 24:9
help, and the **orphan** who had no helper	Job 29:12
And the **orphan** has not shared it	Job 31:17
he grew up with me as with a father	Job 31:18
lifted up my hand against the **orphan**	Job 31:21
have been the helper of the **orphan**	Ps. 10:14
vindicate the **orphan** and the oppressed	Ps. 10:18
Defend the **orphan**, Plead for the widow	Isa. 1:17
They do not defend the **orphan**	Isa. 1:23
the cause, the cause of the **orphan**	Jer. 5:28
the alien, the **orphan**, or the widow	Jer. 7:6
the stranger, the **orphan**, or the widow	Jer. 22:3
For in You the **orphan** finds mercy	Hos. 14:3

do not oppress the widow or the **orphan**	Zech. 7:10
in his wages, the widow and the **orphan**	Mal. 3:5

Orphans (10)

would even cast *lots* for the **orphans** And	Job 6:27
strength of the **orphans** has been crushed	Job 22:9
drive away the donkeys of the **orphans**	Job 24:3
the stranger and murder the **orphans**	Ps. 94:6
pity on their **orphans** or their widows	Isa. 9:17
And that they may plunder the **orphans**	Isa. 10:2
Leave your **orphans** behind, I will keep	Jer. 49:11
We have become **orphans** without a father	Lam. 5:3
"I will not leave you as **orphans**	John 14:18
visit **orphans** and widows in their distress	James 1:27

Fatherless (6)

the **fatherless** and a judge for the widows	Ps. 68:5
Vindicate the weak and **fatherless**	Ps. 82:3
be gracious to his **fatherless** children	Ps. 109:12
He supports the **fatherless** and the widow	Ps. 146:9
Or go into the fields of the **fatherless**	Prov. 23:10
the **fatherless** and the widow they have	Ezek. 22:7

Adoption (5)

of **adoption** as sons by which we cry out	Rom. 8:15
waiting eagerly for *our* **adoption** as sons	Rom. 8:23
to whom belongs the **adoption** as sons	Rom. 9:4
we might receive the **adoption** as sons.	Gal. 4:5
He predestined us to **adoption** as sons	Eph. 1:5

Children of God (3)

power to become the **children of God**	John 1:12
our spirit, that we are the **children of God**	Rom. 8:16
that we should be called **children of God**	1 John 3:1

Heirs

    heirs of God, and joint-**heirs** with Christ   Rom. 8:17

Illegitimate (2)

    No one of **illegitimate** birth shall enter   Deut. 23:2

    you are **illegitimate** children and not sons   Heb. 12:8

Lonely

    God places the **lonely** in <u>families</u>   Ps. 68:6

Appendix G

Recommended Reading

Starting and Growing Your Church Adoption Ministry
www.hfgf.org > Ministry resources > Adoption Ministry Manual,
to download a free e-copy.

Adopted for Life by Russell D. Moore
http://www.crossway.org/books/adopted-for-life-tpb/

Journey to the Fatherless by Lawrence E. Bergeron
www.journeytothefatherless.com

"Abba Changes Everything:" *Christianity Today*, July 2010, pg. 20 by
Russell D. Moore
www.ctlibrary.com/ct/2010/july/10.18.html.

The Adoption Network by Laura Christianson

The Adoption Decision by Laura Christianson

Fields of Fatherless by C. Thomas Davis

Secure in God's Embrace, Living as the Father's Adopted Child by Ken Fong

Adopting for Good: A Guide for People Considering Adoption by Jorie Kincaid

The Whole Life Adoption Book by Jayne E. Schooler

Twenty Things Adoptive Kids Wish Their Adoptive Parents Knew by
Sherrie Eldridge

Twenty Life-Transforming Choices Adoptees Need to Make by Sherrie Eldridge

About the Author

Gerald's military career as a U.S. Air Force pilot led him to the Philippines numerous times. Little did he know then that twenty-six years later he would be living in the Philippines for six years, but God already had plans for his future in the Philippines.

That's where He gave Gerald the equivalent of a six-year graduate course in orphanology while working with children in a mission orphanage, from 1996 - 2002. That experience shattered his traditional image of an orphanage and left him wondering, "What's wrong with this picture?" His inability to answer his own question challenged Gerald to search for a Bible study about orphan ministry and adoption, but he soon discovered that no such resource existed. That caused him to dig deep into the Bible for a Godly model of orphan care, and this book is the ultimate result of his research. The first edition was published on line in 2005, and the book has continued to grow and develop until now.

Gerald learned from countless heart breaking personal experiences that a new paradigm for orphan ministry was urgently needed, and has chosen to devote the rest of his life to speaking and teaching about adoption as a ministry of the church, and to helping families adopt. While serving as business administrator for the orphanage, Gerald discovered that adoption is far more cost-effective than institutional care, especially when children are adopted by families in their own country and culture!

Gerald and his wife now live in beautiful Southern Oregon, and have been speaking, teaching and advocating for adoption as ministry since 1997. In 2003 they established the Home For Good Foundation that has enabled them to share their vision with thousands of others. Quite a number of them are now conducting adopting adoption ministries in their own churches, and some are beginning to follow Gerald's vision to plant adoption ministries in evangelical churches around the world.

Home for Good Foundation

Member: Christian Alliance for Orphans

The author is listed on the Speakers Bureau of the Christian Alliance for Orphans.

http://www.christianallianceforororphans.org/speakers/gerald-clark/

Home for Good Foundation (USA)
www.hfgf.org
adopt@hfgf.org

Philippines
www.homeforgood.org.ph
adoptionministry2011@gmail.com

Uganda
signofthedoveug@gmail.com

What Your Support Will Accomplish

Your contributions to the Home for Good Foundation will empower us to donate more copies of this Bible study to seminary libraries, and to pastors in churches around the world. Several thousand free copies have already been distributed in Africa, India, the Philippines, and other countries. It also allows us to send speakers to teach about adoption ministry in churches where they can't afford to pay a speaker. We focus our efforts on engaging and equipping others to undertake adoption ministries in their own church, and allow God to multiply our efforts. This has resulted in numerous adoption ministries in churches in several countries, where thousands of children have already been adopted. We believe that our ministry model is the most cost effective way to accomplish the maximum return on investment. Rather than funding and doing all the ministries ourselves, we train and equip others to fund and to establish the same self-replicating model in their own churches.

Speakers Available

Gerald and his wife, Maureen, are available to speak in your church about adoption and the gospel, and adoption as a part of the global mission strategy of your church. We also have a staff missionary in the Philippines who is eager to speak in your church. In Uganda, our missionary pastor is available to travel throughout Africa to speak about African families adopting children in their own country and culture.